The Gospel of the Church's Infancy

The Gospel
of the
Church's Infancy

by the REV. J. P. CHARLIER, O. P.

Translated by John L. Sullivan

ST. NORBERT ABBEY PRESS
De Pere, Wisconsin
U.S.A.
1969

Edited by Lisa McGaw

Translated by John L. Sullivan

Originally published as *L'Evangile de L'Enfance de L'Eglise* by La Oensee Catholique, Brussels, Belgium.

Standard Book Number 8316-1030-1
Library of Congress Catalog Card Number 78-87813

Printed in the United States of America
ST. NORBERT ABBEY PRESS
De Pere, Wisconsin 54115

CONTENTS

ACTS OF THE APOSTLES

In the former book, O Theophilus, I spoke of all that Jesus did and taught from the be-
2 ginning / until the day on which he was taken up, after he had given commandments through the Holy Spirit to the apostles whom he had
3 chosen. To them also he showed himself alive after his passion by many proofs, during forty days appearing to them and speaking of the king-
4 dom of God. And while eating with them, he charged them not to depart from Jerusalem, but to wait for the promise of the Father, "of which
5 you have heard," said he, "by my mouth; for John baptized with water, but you shall be baptized with the Holy Spirit not many days hence."

6 They therefore who had come together began to ask him, saying, "Lord, wilt thou at this time restore the kingdom to Israel?"

7 But he said to them, "It is not for you to know the times or dates which the Father has fixed by
8 his own authority; but you shall receive power when the Holy Spirit comes upon you, and you shall be witnesses for me in Jerusalem and in all Judea and Samaria and even to the very ends of the earth."

9 And when he had said this, he was lifted up

before their eyes, and a cloud took him out of
10 their sight. And while they were gazing up to
11 heaven as he went, behold, two men stood by
them in white garments, and said to them, "Men
of Galilee, why do you stand looking up to
heaven? This Jesus who has been taken up from
you into heaven, shall come in the same way as
you have seen him going up to heaven."

12   Then they returned to Jerusalem from the
mount called Olivet, which is near Jerusalem, a
13 Sabbath day's journey. And when they had
entered the city, they mounted to the upper room
where were staying Peter and John, James and
Andrew, Philip and Thomas, Bartholomew and
Matthew, James the son of Alpheus, and Simon
14 the Zealot, and Jude the brother of James. All
these with one mind continued steadfastly in
prayer with the women and Mary, the mother of
Jesus, and with his brethren.

15   In those days Peter stood up in the midst of
the brethren (now the number of persons met
together was about a hundred and twenty), and
16 he said, "Brethren, the Scripture must be fulfilled
which the Holy Spirit declared before by the
mouth of David concerning Judas, who was the
17 guide of those who arrested Jesus; inasmuch as
he had been numbered among us and was allotted
18 his share in this ministry. And he indeed bought
a field with the price of his iniquity and, being
hanged, burst asunder in the midst, and all his
19 bowel gushed out. And it became known to all

the residents of Jerusalem, so that the field came
to be called in their language Haceldama, that is,
20   the Field of Blood. For it is written in the book
of Psalms.

> 'Let their habitation become desolate
>   and let there be none to dwell in it.'

And,

> 'His ministry let another take.'

21   "Therefore, of these men who have been in
our company all the time that the Lord Jesus
22   moved among us, / from John's baptism until the
day that he was taken up from us, of these one
must become a witness with us of his resurrection."

23   And they put forward two: Joseph called
Barsabbas, who was surnamed Justus, and Mat-
24   thias. And they prayed and said, "Thou, Lord,
who knowest the hearts of all, show which of
25   these two thou hast chosen / to take the place
in this ministry and apostleship from which Judas
fell away to go to his own place."

26   And they drew lots between them, and the
lot fell upon Matthias; and he was numbered with
the eleven apostles.

ACTS OF THE APOSTLES

1   And when the days of Pentecost were drawing
to a close, they were all together in one place.
2   And suddenly there came a sound from heaven,
as of a violent wind blowing, and it filled the
3   whole house where they were sitting. And there
appeared to them parted tongues as of fire, which
4   settled upon each of them. And they were all
filled with the Holy Spirit and began to speak in
foreign tongues, even as the Holy Spirit prompted
them to speak.

5   Now there were staying at Jerusalem devout
6   Jews from every nation under heaven. And when
this sound was heard, the multitude gathered
and were bewildered in mind, because each heard
7   them speaking in his own language. But they
were all amazed and marvelled, saying, "Behold,
are not all these that are speaking Galileans?
8   And how have we heard each his own language
9   in which he was born? Parthians and Medes and
Elamites, and inhabitants of Mesopotamia, Judea,
10   and Cappadocia, Pontus and Asia, / Phrygia and
Pamphylia, Egypt and the parts of Libya about
11   Cyrene, and visitors from Rome, / Jews also and
proselytes, Cretans and Arabians, we have heard
them speaking in our own languages of the
wonderful works of God."

12 And all were amazed and perplexed, saying
13 to one another, "What does this mean?" But
others said in mockery, "They are full of new
wine."

14 But Peter, standing up with the Eleven, lifted
up his voice and spoke out to them: "Men of
Judea and all you who dwell in Jerusalem, let this
be known to you, and give ear to my words.
15 These men are not drunk, as you suppose, for it
16 is only the third hour of the day. But this is what
was spoken through the prophet Joel:

17   'And it shall come to pass in the last days,
              says the Lord,
          that I will pour forth of my Spirit upon all
              flesh;
          And your sons and your daughters shall
              prophesy,
              and your young men shall see visions,
              and your old men shall dream dreams.

18   And moreover upon my servants and upon
              my handmaids
              in those days will I pour forth of my Spirit,
              and they shall prophesy.
19   And I will show wonders in the heavens
              above
              and signs on the earth beneath,
              blood and fire and vapor of smoke.
20   The sun shall be turned into darkness, and
              the moon into blood,

Before the day of the Lord comes, the great
and manifest day.

21   And it shall come to pass
That whoever calls upon the name of the
Lord shall be saved.'

22   "Men of Israel, hear these words. Jesus of
Nazareth was a man approved by God among
you by miracles and wonders and signs, which
God did through him in the midst of you, as you
23   yourselves know. Him, when delivered up by
the settled purpose and foreknowledge of God,
you have crucified and slain by the hands of
24   wicked men. But God has raised him up, having
loosed the sorrows of hell, because it was not
25   possible that he should be held fast by it. For
David says with reference to him.

'I saw the Lord before me always,
because he is at my right hand, lest I be
moved.

26   This is why my heart has made merry and my
tongue has rejoiced;
Moreover my flesh also will rest in hope,
27   because thou wilt not abandon my soul to
hell,
neither wilt thou let thy Holy One undergo
decay.
28   Thou hast made known to me the ways of
life;
Thou wilt fill me with joy in thy presence.'

29   "Brethren, let me say to you freely of the

patriarch David that he both died and was buried,
30   and his tomb is with us to this very day. Therefore, since he was a prophet and knew that God
'had sworn to him with an oath that of the fruit
of his loins one should sit upon his throne,' /
31   he, foreseeing it, spoke of the resurrection of the
Christ. For neither was he abandoned to hell,
32   nor did his flesh undergo decay. This Jesus God
has raised up, and we are all witnesses of it.
33   Therefore, exalted by the right hand of God, and
receiving from the Father the promise of the
Holy Spirit, he has poured forth this Spirit which
34   you see and hear. For David did not ascend into
heaven, but he says himself,

'The Lord said to my Lord:
Sit thou at my right hand,
35   until I make thy enemies
thy footstool.'

36   "Therefore, let all the house of Israel know
most assuredly that God has made both Lord and
Christ, this Jesus whom you crucified."

37   Now on hearing this they were pierced to the
heart and said to Peter and the rest of the apostles, "Brethren, what shall we do?"

38   But Peter said to them, "Repent and be baptized every one of you in the name of Jesus Christ
for the forgiveness of your sins; and you will re-
39   ceive the gift of the Holy Spirit. For to you is
the promise and to your children and to all who

are far off, even to all whom the Lord our God calls to himself."

40   And with very many other words he bore witness, and exhorted them, saying, "Save yourselves from this perverse generation."

41   Now they who received his word were baptized, and there were added that day about three thousand souls.

42   And they continued steadfastly in the teaching of the apostles and in the communion of the
42   breaking of the bread and in the prayers. And fear came upon every soul; many wonders also and signs were done by means of the apostles in
44   Jerusalem, and great fear came upon all. And all who believed were together and held all
45   things in common, and would sell their possessions and goods and distribute them among all
46   according as anyone had need. And continuing daily with one accord in the temple, and breaking bread in their houses, they took their food with
47   gladness and simplicity of heart, praising God and being in favor with all the people. And day by day the Lord added to their company such as were to be saved.

FOREWORD

This book is not set forth as a scientific commentary on the first two chapters of the Acts of the Apostles. It lacks the style and the form of a scientific work. It is also devoid of scientific pretension. This is not to say that it is completely lacking in ambition. What author lacks that?

This book is the final outcome of a thorough study which has been both critical and Christian. As critical, it has not sought to skirt difficulties—indeed, if I am to take some of my colleagues at their word, I might sooner be accused of creating them! In an attempt to resolve these difficulties, this study has made use of the resources of contemporary exegesis. Sacred hermeneutics has at its disposal today tools which, though sharp, are difficult to manipulate. I would beg the clemency of the readers if, unwillingly and unwittingly, the scalpel of my exegesis has injured a text, and I would hope they forgive the clumsy surgeon I had been.

This is a Christian work as well. Long enthralled by these pages of the New Testament which call forth the image of the Church in the mystery of her origins, in the freshness of her first years, I have dealt lovingly with her and I do not deem it unseemly that my love shines forth through the commentary.

As regards the text,[1] I have risked using my own

quite literal translation, with verse-by-verse commentary. This is the driest part of the work, but I believe
it inevitable. Notes after every important pericope
give a synthetic and synoptic view of the various
problems considered.

Typographical exigencies have prevented the inclusion of the customary bibliographical references
with the Notes. Stripped of such bibliographical
material the book may seem indecent to devotees of
exegetical publications. But it is not for their benefit
this book was written. Rather, it is for those Christians who would like to learn more about Scripture
and who seek a guide that will not crush them. For
any who might wish to further their study of what
has merely been sketched here, I have included a
short Bibliography at the end of the book. It is
hardly equitable toward those to whom I am indebted,
but I could not give in to the temptation of terrifying
the reader by burdening him with the list of about
250 names that such equity would require. I trust that
the few indications offered here will be sufficient
invitation for all who wish further to explore these
pages of Scripture.

> J. P. Charlier, O.P.
> La Sarte (Huy)—Montpellier
> October 1963—February 1965

INTRODUCTION

Perhaps due to its position, cramped between the Gospels and the works of Paul, Acts has not always known the favor it enjoys today. The flavor of the Gospels and the doctrinal wealth of the Epistles tended to eclipse this manual of church history, considered interesting rather than useful to Christian holiness. Fortunately this simplistic notion is being corrected, and the Acts of the Apostles is gradually becoming the most studied book of the New Testament.

Acts is primarily a history, not because this was its original intent, but because it is an account of the origin and development of the Church in the first thirty years of its existence. Whatever liberties Luke took with chronology, whatever vagueness or subtlety he used in dealing with certain events, however great the influence of his theology upon his view and his narration of church history, the fact is that the beginning of this work is a documentation, a catalogue of events of rare value to the historian. This second volume of Luke's work is a priceless panorama of the early Church. It stands at the gateway to the entire New Testament, all of whose books were created in milieux described in Acts or similar to them.

Acts is comparable from this viewpoint to the work of the Deuteronomist and of the Chronicler, which furnished a history and a theology of history for the Church of Israel, to which the prophetic writings, the

legislative codices, and the Wisdom literature later
became attached. These "historical" books are the best
way of access to the remainder of the Old Testament
precisely because they give the historical situation.
The same is virtually true of Acts, and any study of
the New Testament should begin here.

The value of Acts is not limited to its historical
interest. It is also a book of theology, as will become
evident in the commentary and be recalled in the
Conclusion. Beyond the event-centered annals of the
early Church, Luke intended to write a "prophetic"
history, as this word was used in Israel to describe
books like Samuel and Kings. How could it be otherwise, since this second volume dedicated to Theophilus
is linked inextricably to the first?

The narrow bond between Acts and the third
Gospel reveals the basic notion which directed their
composition: the Church is Jesus Christ, continued and
lived. This profession of faith subtends the theology
of Acts. It is proclaimed on every page, so to speak,
in diverse manners by various literary devices. As
often as possible Luke underscores the strict parallel
between Gospel and Church situations. Christian
preachers in Acts speak the speeches Jesus had spoken
in the Gospel—compare, for instance, the kerygma
announced by Philip to the eunuch (Acts 8:26-39) or
Peter's discourse, with the conversation between Jesus
and the pilgrims of Emmaus (Luke 24:18-27). Some of
Peter's miracles are modeled upon the Master's.
Stephen's martyrdom immediately recalls the Lord's.
These are all simple but effective literary devices

which translate the same conviction: the Church is Jesus continued.

Acts is the gospel, the Good News of the Church. This commentary is written in the light of this definition. It deals with somewhat less than two chapters of Luke's work, but they are not the least important chapters. Their importance derives from their subject, the mystery of the Church's beginnings. The way in which these origins are presented gives rise to several difficulties. None of the major events described here (Ascension, election of Matthias, Pentecost) may be read without several questions being raised. The uniqueness of these accounts, their particular style, the contradictions brought to light by the examination of parallel passages, the sense of mystery and of wonder deriving from them—all create a problem, one with parallels in the first two chapters of Luke's Gospel.

Simply to determine the literary form of these chapters, as interesting as that might be, offers no solutions satisfactory to theologian or to historian. I have tried to discover a solution which gives the fullest measure of justice to Luke's own intention. It seems to me that the key to this solution is found in the assertion made earlier: in Acts, Luke judges everything, speaks of everything from the viewpoint of the Church rather than from Jesus' viewpoint. The paschal mystery, for instance, expressed in the Gospel as the glorious culmination of Jesus' life, is announced in Acts as the birthplace in mystery of the Church. This divergence in perspective, which seems trivial at first glimpse, helps to clarify several points. The Notes further on, especially those on the Ascension and on Judas' death, will support this exegesis.

It is customary to devote several of the opening paragraphs of a commentary to the problems of authenticity, date, dedication, and place of composition of the work studied. We cannot pause here for such discussions, although we are aware that it is not the best form to proceed on simple affirmations. Works of a more technical nature, their titles included in the Bibliography, will furnish to whoever may feel them necessary the argumentations lacking here.

As I have stated, I consider the Acts of the Apostles to be the work of Luke, author of the third Gospel and companion to Paul. Whatever emendations his work may have undergone, whatever interventions may have been made by other hands bear only upon details. Luke had at his disposal as background material a vast, varied, and generally genuine documentation, including eyewitness accounts, records of personal contacts, and the recollection of the traditions of local churches. Some of these had doubtless been set in writing prior to the composition of Acts, and it is possible Luke used them without feeling it necessary to preserve them as they were, without emendation. On this point, each pericope poses a particular problem with a particular solution.

A word must be said concerning the original language of this book. It seems that the theories about an Aramaic original for all or part of the first fifteen chapters of Acts have had their day. There is no doubt that Luke composed this work in his own tongue, Greek. This does not preclude the possibility of the pre-existence of Aramaic documents which he may have used, nor does such a concession suggest that similar solutions exist for every supposedly "Semitic" section. Moreover, the expression "Semitic" ought to be replaced by "Septuagintal"—deliberately imitative of the Septuagint. We would be well advised to study the Septuagint in order to explain any pericope which thus betrays its intent, its spirit, and its source.

Controversy regarding the composition date of Acts is also on the wane. Catholic exegetes are coming to agree on the probability of a fairly early date, about A.D. 80. There are no serious arguments against such a date. Eusebius' opinion, long favored by Catholic commentators, that the abrupt ending of Acts suggests a date prior to Paul's martyrdom, is based upon a misunderstanding of the basic purpose of Luke, who wished to show the Christian message being brought to the very heart of the empire, there to witness to the hostility of the previously chosen people. Universalism was already a characteristic of the third Gospel. Once Paul was in Rome, Luke's purpose was accomplished and he could lay down his pen in peace.

Title

The most frequent title given to this book is **Acts of Apostles,** with no article. The manuscript tradition is quite hesitant, however, offering at times an abbreviated title—**Acts,** no more—and at times one which is too precise—**Acta Omnium Apostolorum,** "The Acts of all the Apostles," referred to in the Muratorian Canon, ca. 180. Such hesitancy makes this title suspect. Indeed, it is quite certainly inauthentic. The third Gospel also lacked a title, and there is every reason to believe it formed a single volume with Acts. It was apparently when an attempt was made to gather the four Gospels into a single codex, or scroll, that they were assigned the authors' names ascribed to them in oral tradition. It was necessary by the very fact to attribute a title to the second volume of Luke's work. Both separation and titling occurred early, no doubt by the middle of the second century. This form of title is not unique in Hellenistic literature, although it does not follow the more classical rules, which would have preferred a genitive referring to the author to one referring to the principal characters. Otherwise, we should read "The Acts of Luke concerning Apostles." But this is a minor consideration.

It should be noted, finally that the Greek word $\pi\rho\alpha\xi\iota\varsigma$ used here never has, in Luke's works, the meaning "act, action, activity," but always "practice,

custom" (Luke 23:51; Acts 19:18). As for the word
"apostles," it is not restricted to the Twelve, of whom
only Peter and John appear, but refers to all missionaries of the Good News.

Dedication (1:1-2)

VERSE 1   *Thus:* This conjunction is the author's
attempt to translate the particle $\mu\epsilon\nu$ which opens this
long sentence. At the beginning of the apodosis we
should expect to find the correlative $\delta\epsilon$, "and now
. . ." But the second particle is missing, as is often
the case in Luke's works.

In the . . . book I spoke: This is polished Greek,
taking the word $\lambda o\gamma os$ in the most classical sense,
"book," and using the aorist middle ($\epsilon\pi o\iota\eta\sigma\alpha\mu\eta\nu$), quite
rare in the New Testament but very elegant. This
style betrays the perfect Hellenist Luke is.

former: The adjective $\pi\rho\omega\tau os$ usually designates
the first of a long series, i.e., of more than two. In
this instance a purist would have preferred $\pi\rho o\tau\epsilon\rho os$,
"the former." Some commentators have concluded
from this that Acts was not Luke's final work. A third
volume might be lost today, or else Luke, having
planned it, may never have written it. This would
explain the abrupt ending of Acts, which fails to give
the outcome of Paul's trial at Rome. This is requiring
too much of the text, though. Actually, Greek had
come to equate the two adjectives in practice, just as
modern English usage rarely distinguishes between
"first" and "former." Moreover, Luke allows himself
the use of one term for the other in several instances
(cf. Acts 7:12; 12:10).

O Theophilus: It was he to whom the Gospel had been addressed (Luke 1:3). In the attempts to discover his identity a number of theories have been proposed. One recent commentary on Acts suggests that this was a pseudonym of Emperor Domitian's cousin, Flavius Clemens, put to death by his imperial relative in A.D. 95 for his Christian faith. It would be superflous to list these several theories here, as they all leave us in the dark, finally, as to the actual identity of Theophilus, who must remain for us "an illustrious unknown." He may even be a fictitious person, the creation of Luke's literary art.

Having read his name in the Prologue of the Gospel, we should not be surprised to see it repeated here. The best classical usage required that the name of the addressee be mentioned not only at the beginning of each major section of a work, but again in the conclusion of the final section. Theophilus is not greeted a third time at the end of Acts, an omission used by proponents of the existence of a third volume of Luke's work as further evidence in support of their thesis. There are exceptions to this rule though, and it would be fruitless, as we have said, to belabor the text.

all that: ων: a splendid example of the attraction of the relative pronoun, and another classical construction conforming to the language and style of the evangelist, who uses it eleven times in the Gospel and twenty-two times in Acts.

began:[2] This ponderous and unexpected construction requires attention and explanation. It may recall

Luke's intention, stated in the Gospel, to set down all the activities of Jesus "from the beginning" (Luke 1:2) i.e., from Jesus' baptism by John (cf. Acts 10:37). If so, the expression is awkward to say the least. But the translation "all that Jesus did and taught from the beginning" is grammatically impossible. Greater justice would be done the text if it were considered a deliberate imitation of the Septuagint, which made frequent use of this expression following the Hebrew (cf. Genesis 11:6; 41:54; Joshua 3:7; 1 Samuel 3:2; etc.).

This may be a reference to the end of the first page of Genesis, literally translated "and he ceased from all his works which God began to do" (Genesis 2:3). If by this identity of style and expression Luke intends to recall this passage, he also reveals his own plan. The Gospel, which ends here, has been the account of the new creation wrought by Jesus Christ. In the remainder of the work, Luke will attempt to show the gradual peopling of this renewed world in which both God and men are at work.

to do, to teach: A worldly expression recalling the "words and deeds" describing Moses' activity (Acts 7:22). The style of an introductory sentence such as this one calls for emphasis. Priority is given to "do" either because action, being more concrete, is more important than instruction to the Semite, or because the salvation wrought by Jesus is perceived first as an event, a deed, before being considered as a doctrine. Again, it may be merely that the rhythm of the Greek sentence calls for this word order. The two verbs are linked closely by the conjunction τε καί, itself emphatic. This term is rarely used elsewhere in the New Testament—two instances in Matthew, none in Mark, one in John—but it is characteristic of Acts.

VERSE 2   *after he had given commandments:* Luke, not given to wordiness, sees no need to reveal what commandments are referred to. But if we recall the original context, the end of the third Gospel, we may understand more readily. The phrase evidently refers to the worldwide preaching of the Good News (Luke 24:47), the object of this second volume. This was well understood by the witnesses of the manuscript tradition, who allowed the following gloss, "And he commanded them to preach the gospel." We might mention as further evidence the fact that in the only other use of this verb in Acts (13:47), its grammatical object is a quotation from Isaiah 49:6 referring to the universality of mission. The final words of this quotation are soon to be recalled (verse 8).

through the Holy Spirit: The object is instrumental—by the action of the Holy Spirit. In the Greek, the position of this phrase is ambiguous. It is not clear whether it is the command to preach which is given through the Holy Spirit or the choice of the apostles which is effected by his action. There is not necessarily a conflict, and there may be no need to clear up the ambiguity. As is often the case, it may be deliberate. Nonetheless, the grammarian would judge that the phrase bears primarily upon the command given, secondarily upon the choice of the Twelve.

chosen: The verb εκλεγομαι is quite Lucan. Of the twenty-two instances of it in the New Testament, eleven appear in Luke's works. This is the verb he uses in reference to the election of the Twelve (Luke 6:13), of the replacement for Judas (Acts 1:24), and of the seven deacons (Acts 6:5).

he was taken up: There is much to be said about this verb, normally used in reference to the Lord's Ascension (Acts 1:11, 22; Mark 16:9). For now it will suffice to mention the use of the passive which, here as so often in the language of the Septuagint, expresses indirectly the action of God, whose name the author always hesitates to mention. Properly speaking this text refers to Jesus' **assumption,** for it is not by his own power but the Father's that he is raised into heaven.

Synthesis

This introductory sentence reproduces exactly the style of the one which opened the Gospel (Luke 1:1-3). Both conform perfectly to the literary techniques of the era. The now classic reference to the Prologue of the **Treatise on Medicine** of Dioscorides —a Middle Eastern physician and contemporary of Luke—is sufficient to prove it. This sentence artfully works the bond with the conclusion of the Gospel, recalling two of its elements, the instructions to the apostles and the subsequent Ascension. It respects the rules of recapitulation (**anakephalaiosis**) required by the stylistics of the times. This brief summation is not followed, at first glimpse at least, by the outlined introduction to the new work which might have been expected. But this omission must not be over-emphasized, as what follows will indicate.

The theological tone of Acts has now been set. Having recounted in the first book the birth of the new creation, Luke goes on now to the peopling, the development, and the organization of this reborn creation. Indirectly, but nonetheless clearly, the true subject of Acts has been indicated. The object of the former volume had been the ministry of Jesus. That of the latter will be the fulfillment by the apostles of his final instructions, given to them through the action of the Holy Spirit. Henceforth, we foresee, the central character of this book is to be that same Spirit of Jesus, who has directed both the choice of the actors and the staging of the preaching of the Good News throughout the world.

I

THE ASCENSION,
PRELUDE AND GUARANTEE
OF PENTECOST (1:3-12)

The Prior Apparitions (1:3-8)

VERSE 3   *To them also:* οις και: This typically
Lucan expression is often to be repeated (Acts 1:11;
7:45; 10:39; 11:30; etc.).

alive: Whenever speaking of the Resurrection,
Luke insists upon the notion of life. He had done so
previously in the Gospel (24:5, 23). In Acts, this
insistence bears both upon the Lord's Resurrection
(cf. 25:19) and that of Christians like Dorcas who
are associated with it (9:41). It is also quite possible
that such an expression was used as a confession of
faith in Christ. Festus' manner of speaking (Acts
25:19) gives reason to believe so.

passion: The expression used is the aorist infinitive
of the verb παοχω, to suffer. The absolute use of this
verb, without modifiers, is characteristic Lucan usage
in reference to the Passion, i.e., the sufferings and
death of the Lord. Practically, the verb has for Luke
the signification "to die in suffering" (cf. Luke 22:15;
24:46; Acts 3:18; 17:3).

proofs: The word τεκμηριον (**hapax**, **NT**) is used

here in reference to a tangible, palpable, irrefutable proof. This is suggested by the etymological stem τεκμαρ, which designates a marker at the edge of a field, a boundary stone. In medical terminology it had come to mean "obvious symptom." At the beginning of this book, which is to deal with witness borne to Jesus' Resurrection, Luke insists, justifiably, upon the basis and validity of that witness. He will bring up the point again shortly. What he is not about to do is to reveal the nature of this obvious proof, though the immediate context, linked to the end of the Gospel (Luke 24:39, 43), leaves no doubt. Luke is referring to the apparitions, particularly the meals shared with the Risen One.

forty days: More detailed information about this figure and its significance are found in the Note on the Ascension below. Here it will suffice to remark that Acts is the only book of the New Testament which mentions an interval of forty days between the Lord's Resurrection and the events which are the proper object of this book. There is an obvious parallel with the opening of the third Gospel. Luke had mentioned then a similar six-week period between Jesus' baptism by John and the beginning of his preaching of the Good News, object of the first part of the work (Luke 4:1). Such a parallel must be deliberate. It invites the reader to consider this opening page of Acts not only as the historical continuation of the closing page of the Gospel, but also as the theological counterpart of the accounts which began the Good News. The Church's origins are identified with the beginning of Jesus' life. Moreover, the artful composition emphasizes the literary genius of the author.

appearing: The verb οπτανομενος is found nowhere else in the New Testament, and only twice in the Old. The first instance is in 1 Kings 8:8, in reference to the pillars of the Ark which "appeared" from the Holy of Holies in the Temple. The second (Tobit 12:19) is more revealing, since it may be the source of Luke's vocabulary in this passage. When Raphael identifies himself to Tobias and his family before leaving them definitely for heaven, he states, "All these days I did appear to you [ωπτανομην]; I did not eat, nor did I drink, but it was a vision which you saw."

VERSE 4   *While eating with them:* This is an admittedly inadequate translation of the Greek συναλιζομενος, a verb unique in the entire Bible, formed from the stem αλs, "salt." Etymologically, the word means "to share the same salt." In the social life of the Near East, with its hot and thirsty climate, salt is a choice condiment, which a host hastens to give his guests. It has the same role of welcome as the salted biscuits offered in our own culture at cocktail time. Taking the text at the most literal level, one might say that the risen Christ is receiving at his own table. Salt is, in fact, the gift offered by a host to his guests. The nuance which pierces through this polished vocabulary is one of the most intimate friendship shared by those who gather about a common table. The reader must be attentive, for at least three reasons, to these meals shared with the Lord.

First, Luke presents them as indubitable proof of
the reality of the Resurrection. It is characteristic of
his writing to dwell upon the sharing of meals between the apostles and the risen Christ (Luke 24:30,
43; Acts 10:41). Second, there is an exquisite literary
contrast between the forty days of fasting endured
by the Lord at the outset of his public life and these
forty days of feasting between the Resurrection and
the outset of the Church's ministry. Finally, these
love feasts (**agape**) shared from Easter day onward
are rich in doctrine. They are signs that the Kingdom
"comparable to a great feast" has already been in-
augurated.

he charged them: παραγγελλω: a very Lucan verb.
Of the thirty-one instances in the New Testament,
fifteen appear in Luke's works.

not to depart: The verb is in the present infinitive,
which usually connotes duration. A translation conforming to strict grammatical usage would read, "He
charged them not to continue to absent themselves
from Jersualem." An aorist infinitive might have
expressed more adequately the sense required by this
translation. In order to justify the grammatical usage
here preferred by Luke, some commentators have
found it necessary to recall the apparitions in Galilee.
It would be there that the apostle had received the
order no longer to remain absent from the Holy
City. Luke, who has made no reference to these
apparitions, here would betray the use of a source
which had mentioned them. It is more likely, though,

that Luke was using here the language of the **koine**
in which many of the subtleties of classical Greek
grammar had been lost, with the result that the
present tense is used with aorist connotations. Moreover, this injunction merely repeats what Luke had
stated positively in 24:49: "Wait here in the city."
The problem will be dealt with again, indirectly, in
the Note on the plan of Acts.

Jerusalem: Two forms of this noun are found in
the New Testament. One is transliterated from the
Hebrew and cannot be declined. The other is
Hellenized and variable. The second is used here,
but Luke uses the first as well, with no fixed pattern
which might indicate a preference. Some have
observed that the Hebrew form is more current in
the Gospel (27 instances vs. 4 Hellenized) and in the
first part of Acts, which deals mainly with the community in Palestine (26 vs. 7), while the proportion
is reversed in the last thirteen chapters of Acts devoted to Paul's missions (12 Hebrew vs. 18 Greek).
These findings do not authorize in any respect the
conclusion that earlier Aramaic documents underlie
the first three-quarters of Luke's work.

the promise: It is to be explicated in the following verse. The announcement is made by Jesus, but
its object is from the Father. It is the Father's gift,
heralded by the Son. Again this is a transition between the end of the Gospel (Luke 24:49), which
contains the only mention of "promise" in the third
Gospel, and the description of the fulfillment of that
promise on the day of Pentecost (Acts 2:33). It refers

to the gift of the Spirit, toward which the entire account is henceforth to be directed.

which you have heard from my mouth: The transition from narrative form to direct discourse is abrupt and inelegant. This breach of literary taste remains unexplained. It does cast suspicion upon emendations suggested in manuscripts and translations solicitous of linguistic purity.

VERSE 5   *for John . . . Holy Spirit:* The two clauses of this sentence are in strict opposition, both syntactical and theological. The double particle μεν-δε —rendered in French by the repetition of subjects "Jean, lui . . . vous, vous" and suggested in English by the use of the conjunctions "indeed . . . but"— warns of the corresponding theological distinction. This bears first upon the authors of the act of baptism, the Baptist, on the one hand, and, on the other, God, implicit in the use of the passive "You shall be baptized . . . ." The distinction applies as well to the baptisms themselves. The former, John's, was administered **with** water (dative alone) while the second, God's, is given **in** the Holy Spirit (dative with εν). This mode of expression is unique to Luke, who had used it in the Gospel (3:16), while Matthew 3:11 and John 1:26, 31, 33 use two datives with prepositions. In Mark 3:8, two datives without prepositions are used, according to the most reliable texts. Obviously this does not exclude for Luke the use of water in Christian baptism. It does make the function of that water more precise, and reduces its importance. In reality, to become a Christian one must accept being plunged by God into the Holy Spirit, of whom water is but a symbol. Tradition had attributed this prophecy exclusively to John the Baptist (Matthew 3:11 and parallels), but this text, like Acts 11:16, lends it to Jesus himself. The substitution is doubtless due to the change in context. Again, as in the previous verses, we are brought back to the threshold of the Gospel.

VERSE 6   *They, therefore:* οι μεν ουν is a formulation characteristic of Acts. There is not a single instance of it in Matthew, Mark, or John, only one in Luke, but twenty-seven in Acts.

you will restore: The verb is conjugated in the present, but the connotation is of the proximate, almost immediate future. If only by the Gospels, we are aware that contemporary Judaism awaited such a restoration, to be accomplished by the Messiah, considered the singular reincarnation of Elijah (Matthew 17:11) according to the prophecy of Malachi 3:23. It is possible, of course, that Luke is merely translating the down-to-earth expectations of the apostles, even on the morrow of the resurrection. But by his subtle play or irony he also seems to express the true content of his book, the actual description of the inauguration and development of this new and definitive Kingdom.

to Israel: A dative indicating advantage is used rather than the genitive. Israel ought to be at the center of the new Kingdom. Indeed it is to be—"Salvation is from the Jews" (John 4:22)—but in hardly a spectacular manner, bearing little resemblance to traditional expectations.

VERSE 7   *he said to them:* While the New Testament nearly always uses the simple dative in reference to a person spoken to, Luke prefers a preposition followed by the accusative (ειπεν προς αυτους). There are five instances in Matthew, one in Mark, but one hundred in Luke and fifty-three in Acts.

the times or dates: The expression is a cliché, and takes no account of the proper value of the terms. It is also found, in a similar context, in 1 Thessalonians 5:1. Its origin is Daniel 2:21, which attributes power over dates and times to God alone. In referring to it, the Lord is using an argument from Scripture which admits no response.

VERSE 8   *power:* The theme of the Holy Spirit as power is nearly exclusively Lucan. Both in the Gospel and in Acts, Luke speaks of the Spirit as a power, a force (δυναμις). It is the Spirit who sets in motion the work of redemption wrought by Jesus and continued by the Church. It is he who will authenticate it by the miracles (δυναμις), irrefutable signs of their respective missions (cf. Acts 2:22).

It is under the sign of the Spirit of Power that Jesus inaugurates in Galilee, soon after his stay in the desert, the Messianic ministry (Luke 4:14). Henceforth the Spirit will never leave him. It emanates from him at every moment (Luke 6:19). The apostles are assimilated to the Master in this respect. They too perform miracles not by their own power (Acts

3:12) but by a superior strength which never leaves them (Acts 4:33; 6:8).

This promise is expressed here in the same terms as at the end of the Gospel (Luke 24:49). This suggests a more intimate relationship than mere analogy. The promise of the sending of the Spirit of Power had been made in the earliest pages of the Gospel. He it was who was announced to Mary (Luke 1:35). The Incarnation was the act of this Power, this Strength which possessed the Virgin. The verb used to express his coming ($\varepsilon\pi\varepsilon\rho\chi o\mu\alpha\iota$) is the same in the account of the Annunciation and that of Pentecost. In no other instance does this verb have as its subject the Holy Spirit. The analogy is therefore deliberate.

There is, then, a strict parallel between the birth of Jesus and that of the Church. In both instances the Spirit of Power takes possession of the intruments chosen by God for his "coming into the world." By His action Mary gives birth to the physical body of the Lord. Through this same action, the apostles make known the Body of Christ which is the Church. Henceforth the Church is evidently the Body of Christ continued and lived. And the analogy becomes apparent between these opening lines of Acts and the childhood Gospel of which they are the ecclesial parallel.

comes upon you: This is not the verb used to express the gift of the Spirit in the Pentecost account but, as previously mentioned, the one used in the

Annunciation account (Luke 1:35) where it carried echoes of an ancient promise (Isaiah 32:15), the coming of the Spirit which is the promised inaugural of the messianic era.

witnesses: Excepting the Fourth Gospel, Acts is the New Testament book in which this word and its cognates (to witness, to testify, testimony, etc.) are most often used, twenty-nine times in all. This is indeed the book of witness. The word μαρτυς must be taken at full value. It is especially not to be confused with "eyewitness," for which both classical Greek and Luke (1:2) use the term αυτοπτης. This latter word indicates a passive role, the quality described being a matter of fact. The αυτοπτης merely has had the good fortune to be present at an event, and upon occasion if the need be felt or the court require, he may be called upon to render an account of what he has seen, just as he saw it. The μαρτυς has a more active role, a quality beyond that of eyewitness. He has a mission to fulfill, not only to proclaim officially what he has seen, but also to assert its significance, its meaning, its import. Going beyond the event, he becomes the herald—and in a religious context, the theologian—of the message implied by the event. The episode mentioned further on of the replacement of Judas by Matthias illustrates this distinction (Acts 1:15-26). It would not be clear why there should be a choice, an election, a confirmation to institute a witness if he need only have been present at a past event. On the other hand, an election is fully justified if the role of the elect goes beyond this narrow context, if besides his proclamation of the event he must give a correct interpretation of it. The witnesses referred to in Acts are theologians of the salvific action of the Lord.

even to the ends of the earth: The culmination of the program outlined by Jesus is borrowed from the universalist perspectives of Isaiah 49:6. This text had been quoted by Luke at the beginning of the Gospel (2:32) and is to be repeated in Acts 13:47. Luke is quite attentive to underscore the boundless horizon of the Christian message. In the final sentence of this introduction, he suggests artfully the plan of his work. It is a plan one might expect, having read in the first few verses the recapitulation of the Gospel. At this point, the plan requires some further development.

Note 1.   The Plan of the Acts of the Apostles

The plan of Acts is no easier to discern than that of several other biblical or New Testament books. Exegetes are far from complete agreement on the subject. The question is of no little interest, though, as the plan, the general orientation of a work, is often indicative of its preoccupations and purposes. This note does not pretend ambitiously to solve all the problems involved, but it may offer some useful observations.

1.   The Gospel of Luke

The narrow bond uniting Acts with the third Gospel invites a closer look at the first part of Luke's work. It is probable that, one way or another, the basic concept of the former is not unlike that of the latter. Clarification of the basic elements of the Gospel may help to orient the research of those who are studying the account in Acts, since the major concerns of one volume tend to reveal the basic outlines of the other. It should be emphasized, however, that such a procedure does not imply in any manner the logical priority of one plan over the other. The composition of Acts may well have suggested to Luke the outline for his Gospel.

At least in its basic framework, the plan of the Gospel seems fairly substantial. It has a geographic orientation, and Luke makes this geography a theology. Jerusalem is at the topographic center. Here the Gospel account begins and ends. It is precisely in the Temple of Jerusalem, but this notion is already more theological than topographical. The significance of this location is brought out by the difficulties it caused for the evangelist, who needed his talent to avoid the traditional starting points—the Judea of the baptism or of Bethlehem, the Galilee of the beginning of Jesus' ministry—and his freedom of choice to gloss over the Galilean apparitions at the end of the book.

Jesus' entire life is marked by topographical references. The childhood Gospel, a sort of prophetic microgospel of the public life, bears this imprint. After the introduction (Jerusalem), Luke takes us into Judea (Bethlehem), then up into Galilee (Nazareth), only to conclude with a second trip to Jerusalem when Jesus reaches the age of twelve. Similarly, the body of the Gospel takes the Lord into Judea for his baptism, back into Galilee for his early preaching, then finally to Jerusalem at the end of a long journey.

This will to begin and end everything in Jerusalem and in its Temple corresponds to something other than mere geographic concerns. Also, this is less a question of the Judean capital than of the "holy city" of the prophets (Isaiah 52:1), the "city of God" of the psalmist (cf. Psalm 87:3), the city to be freed by Jesus of Nazareth (Luke 2:38). The culmination of these journeys can only be the Temple of Jerusalem wherein, until now, God has dwelt. Henceforth it would be more appropriate to speak of pilgrimages than of journeys. The life of Jesus is directed here by its purpose. His Father's house—the most likely meaning of Luke 2:49—is first of all Jerusalem and, with the transposition imposed by the paschal event, the heavenly Jerusalem of which the earthly city is but a figure. There it is that the glorified Christ completes his journey (Luke 24:51), while the apostles whose own life of ministry is just starting, must remain for a while within the walls of a city and a Temple made by human hands (Luke 24:52).

From this dual orientation, geographical and theological, the Gospel draws its texture and its coherence, expressed though the medium of journeys leading inexorably to Jerusalem, source and end of an activity and of a life drawn there in unceasing pilgrimage.

2. The Acts of the Apostles

Luke responds to a similar concern in the second part of his diptych. The number of journeys and the frequent mention of Jerusalem (63 instances) are convincing enough. Moreover, this purpose is stated in the introduction when Luke outlines the apostolic program: Jerusalem, Judea, Samaria, and the ends of the earth. It would do injury to Luke's intent to reduce this program to mere geographic notation. As in the Gospel, this is a theological concern.

If there is actually a question in the short description of the progressive widening of earthly horizons, one can guess the eventual progress of the gospel announced to men further and further remote from Judaism. Leaving Jerusalem, then Judea, representing orthodox Judaism, the Faithful People, the Good News is borne next into Samaria, the schismatic assembly of Israel, until eventually it reaches the ends of the earth peopled by the **Goyim**, the Gentiles, here represented symbolically by Rome, capital of the empire. Thus the universal character of Christian mission is strongly expressed not merely by the crossing of political frontiers but by the overturning of religious barriers as had been suggested in the oracles of the prophets (cf. Isaiah 48:6; 45:14; etc.).

A short digression comparing Acts with one section of John's Gospel is in order here. The similarity between the plan of Acts and that of John 3-4 is striking. From the viewpoint of theological development, the program is the same in both accounts. In speaking to Nicodemus (John 3:1-21), Jesus is preaching in the capital to orthodox Judaism. After a short ministry, a transitional moment "in the land of Judea" (3:22-26), he confronts adulterous Samaria (4:1-42).

The officer in Capernaum (4:43-54), though residing in Galilee, still represents the Gentile world, at least in the view of the final editor of this section of John's Gospel.

The program Luke sets about to fulfill is a double one. As in John 3-4 there is the theological development, the evangelism of the entire world, Jews first then Gentiles. But this ambition is also geographical. The Good News must resound even to the physical ends of the earth. The first section of the book is concerned with the theological progress, ending when the first Gentiles are, so to speak, officially evangelized. It comprises the first fourteen chapters of the book. There remains the geographical development that is to bring the Gospel to Rome. It is dealt with in chapters 16-28 of Acts. Between the two the so-called Council of Jerusalem stands as a bridge (chapter 15) resolving the problems created by the entry of the Gentiles into the Church, and opening the gateway to allow Paul to become the missionary to the world. The entire book is preceded by a sort of "Gospel of the Childhood of the Church" tracing in two chapters the birth and first steps of the new Kingdom.

The Prologue of Acts, its two sections, and the Council acting as a pivot between them, all have Jerusalem as a setting or as a point of reference. It is from there every mission leaves to bring the program another step forward. It is there that missionaries return at the end of their apostolic journeys. Jerusalem is the city wherein the cross of salvation was raised, and it is therefore from Jerusalem that shall emanate its rays of glory, enlightening the world.

The following synopsis will bring greater clarity to the plan of Acts:

Prologue: Birth of the Church at Jerusalem (1-2)

I.   Theological progress: Jerusalem—Jerusalem (3-14)

      1.   Jerusalem and Judea—orthodox Judaism (3-8:3)

      2.   Samaria—schismatic Judaism (8:4-25)

      3.   Sympathizers with Judaism (8:26-40) Interlude—Saul's conversion (9)

      4.   The Gentiles, evangelized by Peter and by Paul (10-14)

Conclusion of I   }
Introduction of II }   The Council of Jerusalem (15)

II.   Geographical progress (16-28)

      1.   Jerusalem—Jerusalem (15:30-21:26)

      2.   Jerusalem—Rome (21:27-28:31)

To elaborate further upon this plan would require a complete commentary upon Acts. At the conclusion of this book we shall propose, for the Prologue which is its object, some complementary details. For the remainder, a word of explanation must suffice.

On the whole, the progression of the first section of Acts (1-14) is fairly clear. It is necessary, though, to underscore the subdivision of the mission to the Gentiles, which derives from the fact that two missionary journeys are made, respectively, by Peter and by Paul. Paul's role here must be clearly understood. It is Peter who officially opens the gates of the Church to the Gentiles by baptizing Cornelius at Caesarea by the sea. Peter is responsible for the progress of the evangelical work, a fact signified in a way by the mention of Jerusalem at the beginning and end of his journey. Paul, on the other hand, leaves from Antioch and returns there, a sign that his journey adds nothing to what Peter has accomplished. The two missions are described as parallel, Peter's being, in a sense, the model for Paul's. It is during this first voyage from Antioch to Antioch, that Paul pronounces, at Antioch of Pisidia, the only one of his speeches modeled upon the usual plan of Peter's speeches. In a word Paul's missionary journey in Acts 13-14 has no further purpose than to present this neophyte as the designated successor of Peter when, in the second section of Acts, a new herald is needed.

Once the Council had recognized Paul's merits, he could thenceforth be charged with official missions. He became a witness, a μαρτυς, on an equal footing with the Twelve. The task now was given him to extend the Church geographically. A first and unique voyage attempted this, from Jerusalem to Jerusalem, an undertaking which brought the Church's boundaries quite far, but not close enough to the assigned goal. It was undoubtedly necessary for this end, following the Lord's example, to undergo suffering and imprisonment. So it was, paradoxically, by a voyage in chains that the Good News was brought to the capital of the world. Now the immense task begun in the Temple of Jerusalem, where a man struck dumb has listened to the announcement of the Precursor's birth, will be accomplished.

Synthesis

The essential points in verses 3-8 are summarized as follows:

1.   The beginning of Acts is solidly linked with the end of the Gospel, which it recalls. However, one feels that beyond the Ascension to which no reference is made—except the one in verse 2 dealing with it as a past event—the entire account already is oriented toward the mystery of the Church and the coming of the Holy Spirit. Luke had concluded his first volume with the narrative of the paschal mystery, the glorious culmination of Jesus' life. He now recalls the final phases of that mystery, insofar as they inaugurate the life of the Church. These two perspectives, though quite disparate, explain the eventual discrepancies between these two pages of Luke's works, as shall soon be seen in reference to the Ascension.

2.   If the ending of Luke's Gospel and the beginning of Acts coincide, the same may be said of the beginning of the Gospel and that of Acts. Far beyond any resemblances called forth by the two introductory sentences, there is a certain parallel suggested between Jesus' childhood and that of the Church. Both volumes of Luke's work open with a promise coming from the Father and requiring for its fulfillment the intervention of the Spirit of Power.

Both sections mention the themes of universities and of Kingdom. The identity of starting point—Jerusalem —further suggests this parallel, obviously deliberate, and repeated further on.

3.   By including in his account dialogue between Jesus and his disciples, Luke informs the reader indirectly about the object of his work. For it is the planting and the growth of the Kingdom on earth he mentions constantly, and this progress is considered the prelude to the final restoration. In the same intent, he insists upon the meals shared with the risen Christ, as they herald the preparation of the great feast of the Church, wherein the redeemed shall partake of the Lord's table.

4.   These meals shared among the disciples who are rejoicing in the great paschal joy, and prolonged throughout forty days, before the ministry and preaching of the Church began, may also be appreciated from another more literary viewpoint. They represent a beautiful pendant to the forty days of rigorous fasting, lived in solitude and temptation, before Jesus began his ministry and preaching.

5.   This book is heralded as the account of witness borne to the Resurrection, justifying its appeal to tangible, effective proof. But the apostles, left to themselves, were incapable of sure and faithful witness. It was neither permissible nor possible for them to inaugurate the task of evangelization until they had received the new baptism which plunged them into the Spirit of Power. This is why Pentecost is to

be the decisive event of all these acts. It serves as
the frontispiece of this work. All that preceded was
preparation, theological or literary.

6.   Finally, Luke has artfully suggested the plan
of his work, both theological and topographical. It
was the plan of the Gospel account and there, as
here, he had let it be previewed in the childhood
Gospel.

The Ascension (1:9-12)

VERSE 9   *he was raised:* This verb (ἐπαίρω) is used
nowhere else in reference to the Ascension, though
Luke quite often uses it in other contexts (11 instances
in Luke-Acts, but only one in Matthew, none in Mark,
4 in John and 3 in the remainder of the New Testament). Notice again the use of the passive to indicate
an action having God as its author.

took him out of their sight: Exceptionally, the verb
ὑπολαμβάνω, which usually means "to think, to believe," is taken in its literal sense "to raise from below,
to remove."

VERSE 10   *while:* This conjunction has a temporal
sense. Quite rare in the New Testament, it belongs
mainly to Luke's vocabulary.

gazing: This is another Lucan verb. A comparison
with other passages in which he uses it (Luke 4:20;
Acts 3:4) will reveal its precise meaning "to stretch
one's neck, to stare."

and behold: This expression introduces the apodosis of the sentence. Luke uses it often (24 instances

in the Gospel, 8 in Acts). The style is imitative of the Septuagint, which often uses this turn of phrase. It is found notably in the parallel pericope in 2 Kings 2:11, about which more is to be said in the Note on the Ascension. Moreover, this sentence recalls Luke 24:4.

in white garments: White being the color of joy and of heaven, such raiment is obviously required here. It constitutes a sort of heavenly privilege, and is recognized as such in the Old Testament (cf. Daniel 7:9; 2 Maccabees 11:8). It also recalls the description of the Transfiguration (Mark 9:3 and parallels), and that of the angels who announced the Resurrection (Mark 16:5 and parallels).

VERSE 11   *Men of Galilee:* This form of address is elegant Greek. It is a mode of expression unknown in the New Testament outside of Acts, where it is used twenty-two times.

looking up to heaven: Would it be exaggerating to see in this inquiry a deliberate contrast of imagery with the scene of the discovery of the empty tomb in Luke 24:5? Here the apostles gaze toward heaven, where they suppose Jesus has gone, while their attention should be directed toward the world confided to their evangelization. There the women's eyes were fixed upon the earth, beneath which they believed Jesus to be present, in the abode of the dead, while to the contrary the Lord by his Resurrection had entered already the glory of heaven. In both instances angels come with gentle good humor to rectify attitudes falsified by a misunderstanding of events. If the contrast is deliberate it is of great artistic value.

in the same way: The comparison between the two situations, Jesus' Ascension and return, rather awkward by its pleonasm, bears directly, it seems, upon the cloud. However, we shall see further on that it is valid for the entire scene.

VERSE 12   *Olivet:* It seems preferable to read ελαιων, "the Olive Orchard," rather than the genitive plural ελαιων, "of Olives," used by Luke in 22:39.

a Sabbath day's journey: This refers to the distance it was permissible to walk on the Sabbath without breaking the rule of rest, viz., a bit less than one kilometer, about two-thirds of a mile. The notation is strictly spatial, no indication being given of the day of the week on which the event actually occurred.

Note 2.   The Ascension

The short account in Acts raises several problems which may be summarized to three major questions. The first is rather of a literary order. These few are imprinted with a sense of wonder quite rare in the New Testament, but more common in descriptions of theophany. The second is of a more historical nature. The descriptions found here clash with the other New Testament accounts of the Ascension, as will be explained further on. The third is raised by the theologian, who finds it difficult to grasp how the Ascension, understood as the entry of Christ into the glory of the Father, may be chronologically separated from the Resurrection. Is it not by a unique act that Christ frees himself victoriously from death and inherits the glory he had set aside at the Incarnation?

It would be vain and in bad form to gloss over these problems. By confronting them one can learn better to appreciate Luke's narrative art, to discover the internal richness of his account, and to perfect one's knowledge of the mystery he relates. A first part of this Note will recall parallel passages in the New Testament. A second will study the account in Acts. Conclusions of a literary, historical, and doctrinal nature may then be suggested, which will make clear the fundamental unity and coherence of this typically Lucan composition.

1. The Ascension in the New Testament

(excluding Acts)

a. Matthew. The first Gospel ends with no specific mention of the Ascension. After the Resurrection Jesus appears to the women (28:9-10) to tell them to convince the apostles to go up into Galilee. We find them there after a journey which must have taken several days, upon the mountain ($\epsilon\iota\varsigma$ τo $o\rho o\varsigma$, 28:16) where the Lord grants them all power ($\epsilon\xi ov\sigma\iota\alpha$). Despite the definte article, which seeks to make it more precise, this mountain is not otherwise known. It is not at all certain that it can be identified legitimately—with Tabor or Hermon, for instance—as its role is more properly theological or literary than topographical. Theological, as we shall say more explicitly in regard to Acts, because the mountain is the traditional site for the encounter between God and man. Literary, too, because it recalls that other mountain at the beginning of the Gospel upon which Satan had endeavored to confer upon Jesus dominion over all the earth (4:8). Not only is there no reference here to Jesus' Ascension, there is even an impression that the event had occurred already, since Jesus had received all power in heaven and on earth.

b. Mark. Mark's own account ends abruptly with 16:8. Earliest Christian tradition sought to fill this obvious void by making use, apparently, of the canonical Gospels of Matthew and Luke, amalgamated and summarized. In its conclusion, which is inspired, canonical, but inauthentic, Mark's account contains a mention of the Ascension (16:19), consisting of the following three sentence fragments:

"So then the Lord, after he had spoken to them . . .," an introduction which seems either redactional or, more probably, borrowed from Luke, whose style it recalls (ο μεν ουν κυριος . . .);

". . . was taken up into heaven . . .," which repeats word for word the terms of Elijah's assumption (2 Kings 2:11);

". . . and sits at the right hand of God," undoubtedly formed upon the model of Psalm 110:1 "Sit thou on my right hand . . ." based upon a Christological interpretation of this psalm acquired quite early in Christian reflection.

Obviously such a formulation is theological. It

affirms without possible dissent the reality of the Ascension mystery, but it does not engage in any description of the event. There is no chronological benchmark, but it may be assumed that this occurs on the day of the Resurrection (cf. 16:9). Geographically, the locale is equally vague. The order was given in 16:7 to go up into Galilee, but there is no indication it has been carried out, and this could as easily be happening in Jerusalem.

c. Luke.   At the end of his Gospel, Luke makes one brief reference to the Lord's Ascension. By its very conciseness it obviously does not intend to be descriptive. The scene is Bethany, which may coincide ad sensum with the Mount Olivet mentioned in Acts. Beyond this geographical approximation, though, there is not a single common detail between the accounts in Luke and in Acts. Particularly, the Gospel narrative situates the Ascension at the end of the long Easter day.

In the body of the Gospel, Luke had made one rather sybilline reference to Jesus' Ascension. At the moment he undertakes the great journey to Jerusalem, the object of the second part of the Gospel, Luke draws forth from his pen the maximum of pomp and solemnity. In a style strongly imitative of the Septuagint, the evangelist announces Jesus' decision: "Now it came to pass when the days had come for him to be taken up, that he steadfastly set his face to go to Jerusalem . . ." (εγενετο δε εν τω ουμπληρουαθαι τας ημερας της αναλημψεως αυτου και αυτος το προσωπον εοτηρισεν του πορευεσθαι εις Ἰερουσαλημ . . ., 9:51). Two

words are particularly significant, "to be taken up"
(ἀναλημψις) recalling Acts 1:11, where the same stem
(ἀναλαμβανομαι) is used in reference to the Ascension,
and "to go" (πορευεσθαι), which we shall discuss first.
Trivial as it may seem, this verb is, in Luke's usage,
rich in doctrine and deserving of explanation.

"To go" (πορευεσθαι) does not refer to the idea of
an everyday trip, but connotes the notion of pilgrimage. This is obviously how it is to be taken in Luke
2:41, the account of the journey Jesus made at the
age of twelve with Mary and Joseph. That final
episode of the childhood Gospel is merely a stepping
stone, for to the degree that the reader is familiar
with the Old Testament he will recognize that, beyond
the account, this pilgrimage is the prefiguring of
another, to occur later on, which will be otherwise
important and glorious.

The evangelist himself states at the end of his
account, "[Mary] kept all these things carefully in
her heart" (2:51). The Greek ρημα, "word," is taken
here in its vague biblical sense, "event, thing." This
mode of expression is quite common in the Bible.
There are several enlightening examples. Jacob,
while rebuking Joseph for revealing his dreams so
naively, "keeps the thing in his heart" (Genesis 37:11,
author's translation). Daniel, too, after pondering
the great vision, ends the chapter, "As for me, Daniel,
my thoughts greatly troubled me, and my countenance
was changed: but I kept the matter in my heart"
(Daniel 7:28). This is what Nebuchadnezzar had done
when Daniel interpreted the dreams concerning him

(Daniel 4:28, LXX). The evident sense of the expression is this: during dreams, visions, events which foretell superior realities, the seer or person concerned keeps in his heart this "word," to ponder it while awaiting its definitive fulfillment.

So too the Virgin Mary keeps in her heart this first pilgrimage ($\pi o \rho \epsilon \upsilon \epsilon \sigma \theta \alpha \iota$) of her son while awaiting the true pilgrimage, the greater mystery, of which this has been merely the figure and the veiled image. That second journey to Jerusalem is precisely the one which begins in the text quoted above (Luke 9:51). Jesus now is going to fulfill the true liturgy of the new Pasch through which he is to attain his glorification. He now goes up to Jerusalem to offer his own sacrifice, facing the Temple, upon the altar of the Cross. And, as it had occurred when he was twelve, he is to remain lost for three days, before he is found $\epsilon \nu \ \tau o \iota s \ \tau o \upsilon \ \pi \alpha \tau \rho o s \ \mu o \upsilon$, "in my Father's house."

This journey to Jerusalem parallels the one in the Gospel. Heralded in 9:51, it is recalled three times (13:22; 17:11; 19:28) in practically identical terms. But it is, in a sense, merely a terrestrial journey. The goal of the Lord's pilgrimage can only be the celestial Temple wherein his Father dwells. It is normal, then, to find this verb "to go" ($\pi o \rho \epsilon \upsilon \epsilon \sigma \theta \alpha \iota$) one last time in the account of the Ascension in Acts (1:10-11) where the pilgrimage is definitively fulfilled.

These explanations, while somewhat lengthy, are necessary. They allow us to return to the term "to be taken up" ($\alpha \nu \alpha \lambda \eta \mu \psi \iota s$). It is no longer certain that its connotation in Luke 9:51 is restricted to the single act of Ascension. Rather, it would refer to the entire paschal mystery, designating globally the Passion, death, Resurrection, and Ascension, considered as an inseparable unity. All these events constitute the elevation, the exaltation of Jesus. This manner of perceiving and understanding these events shows, as we shall see, how close Luke is to Johannine theology.

At the point of the inquiry it would seem that Luke is hardly concerned with the distinction between the Lord's Resurrection and Ascension. For him, the two mysteries are complementary. Only a literary device, justified by a particular theological perspective —which we have yet to discover—could have brought the writer to divide into two moments the unique mystery of Jesus' glorification, as he has done in the presentation of Acts 1.

d. John. John's theology does not differ essentially from Luke's. It too expresses the realities we are presently concerned with by the use of two verbs. The theology of pilgrimage, represented in Luke by the term "to go" ($\pi o \rho \varepsilon \upsilon \varepsilon \sigma \theta \alpha \iota$), is expressed in John by the verb "to ascend" ($\alpha \nu \alpha \beta \alpha \iota \nu \omega$), a more common usage. When in the Fourth Gospel this verb has Jesus as its subject, it takes one of two objects. Jesus goes up only to Jerusalem or to the Father, the former being the figure of the latter. The theme of Jesus' elevation expressed in Luke by the verb "to be taken up" ($\alpha \nu \alpha \lambda \alpha \mu \beta \alpha \nu o \mu \alpha \iota$), is represented in John by the term "to glorify" ($\delta o \xi \alpha \zeta \omega$), also used in reference to the entire paschal mystery. In their basic outline, then,

Lucan and Johannine theologies are distinguished merely by differences of word usage.

The particular question of the Ascension is not presented differently either. John makes a veiled reference to it in 3:13, and another somewhat clearer one in 6:62, at the end of the discourse on the bread of life. Besides these two affirmations, the evangelist gives no account, no description of the Ascension as distinct from the Resurrection. The only reference to it in the post-paschal accounts is in the episode of the Magdalene, to whom the Risen One says, "Do not touch me, for I have not yet ascended [$\alpha\nu\alpha\beta\epsilon\beta\eta\kappa\alpha$] to my Father, but go to my brethren and say to them, 'I ascend [$\alpha\nu\alpha\beta\alpha\iota\nu\omega$, present tense] to my Father' . . ." (20:17). The tenses used here indicate that this ascension is imminent. According to every hypothesis, it will have occurred when Jesus returns among the Eleven ". . . late that same day" (20:19) to impart the Holy Spirit.

e. Paul.   There is no need to dwell on the Pauline writings. Their literary form—letters—and the apostle's deliberately abstract thought offer little promise of a wealth of concrete detail concerning the Lord's Ascension. Paul undoubtedly knows it and preaches it, but his teaching on the subject is rare and is usually included in the kerygma on the Resurrection. Between these mysteries Paul only occasionally works a completely theological distinction as if he considered Resurrection and Ascension as two inseparable facets of the same reality.

Thus Resurrection and Ascension are mentioned

together in the unique super-exaltation ($\upsilon\pi\epsilon\rho\upsilon\psi\omega\sigma\epsilon\nu$) in the hymn of Philippians 2:9. On the other hand, the christological hymn in 1 Timothy 3:16 reserves a mention, if a modest one, for the assumption into glory of the Savior ($\alpha\nu\epsilon\lambda\eta\mu\phi\theta\eta\ \epsilon\nu\ \delta\sigma\xi\eta$). There is a clearer reference in Ephesians 4:10, where the Ascension is emphasized in its close relationship to the gift of the Spirit. It is omitted, on the other hand, from the letter to the Colossians, where some reference to it might have been expected, as this entire epistle seeks to demonstrate and to preach the brilliant superiority of the exalted Christ over those celestial powers held in such high esteem by the Colossians. Similar remarks might be made concerning Romans 8:34 and 1 Corinthians 15:3-7, two texts strangely silent about a mystery they seem to call forth of themselves.

f. The Remaining New Testament Books. A similar discretion is observed in the other New Testament books. At most there are veiled references to the Ascension in the Epistle to the Hebrews (4:14; 9:11, 24) but these are inspired by the Old Testament (cf. Hebrews 6:19), and do not depart from the general teaching on the Ascension. The reference in 1 Peter 3:22 completes the list. Even the Apocalypse, the book of the glorious Lordship of Jesus in Heaven, is surprisingly silent about the entry into glory of Jesus at his Father's side. It is only in the book of Acts that the account in 1:9-12 is offered as a **hapax.** All other references to the mystery of the Ascension are stated in theological terms which do not differ from the usual presentation in the New Testament (Acts 2:33; 5:31).

Conclusion. In the entire New Testament, as briefly reviewed here, the Ascension is obviously known, mentioned, preached, but as a dogmatic theological fact rather than as an event liable to description. It is not formally distinguished from the Resurrection, or from Christ's sitting at the right hand of the Father. It is presented as a particular facet of the unique jewel which is the paschal mystery.

There are evidently several aspects to that mystery, according to the viewpoint from which it is considered. By his Resurrection, Jesus escaped from death, whose bonds were broken. This is a rather negative aspect. Jesus is no longer dead. By the same Resurrection, he has been glorified, exalted, i.e., he has found anew the glory he had laid aside in the kenosis of the Incarnation—a positive aspect. It is normal to express the second viewpoint, considered independently of the first, in terms antithetic with respect to the Incarnation. If the latter was a "descent" to earth, the former is a re- "ascent" into heaven precisely described by the abstract term "ascension."

There is no reason to be surprised at the apparent reticence of inspired writers in reference to this event of the Ascension. It is undoubtedly authentic, but as ineffable as the Resurrection. No one had seen Christ **rising** and **ascending** into glory. It is solely because he has been seen **risen** that he is known to have **ascended** into the glory of the Father.

There remains to be studied for its own sake the particular presentation Luke makes of the Ascension in the Prologue of this volume on the Church. An effort must be made to define the particular teaching Luke proposes and to set in relief the motives which have prompted him to adopt this rather novel and original form of expression.

2.   The Account in Acts 1:9-12

In reference to the parallel passages, the account in Acts presents a number of original elements relating either to details brought by an eyewitness—which Luke, of course, could not claim to be—or to theological formulae traditional in both Testaments and in which, by definition, the significance surpasses the signification. These elements may be reduced to five:

1.   a chronological detail—40 days (verse 3)
2.   a topographical detail—Mount Olivet (verse 12)
3.   a descriptive detail—the cloud (verse 9)
4.   an explanatory remark—the angels and their discourse (verses 10-11)
5.   a guarantee—the eyewitness (verses 9-11)

The five elements must be studied meticulously in order to discover precisely what Luke intended them to signify.

a.   The Mention of the Forty Days (verse 3). This detail, as we have said, is unique in the entire New Testament in reference to the Ascension. Other witnesses bear upon hardly more than the dogmatic reality. At most, when they make use of another, more historical, literary form, as in the Gospels, they situate the Ascension on Easter day, expressing by the chronological unity the intrinsic unity of the paschal mystery. In Luke and John some interval is suggested between Christ's Resurrection and his return to the Father. But beyond the fact that this detail is not supported by emphasis, we must bear in mind the difficulty encountered by the Semite in expressing absolute simultaneity. For him it is a common procedure to suggest logical distinctions by making chronological divisions. From the moment of his Resurrection, Christ is endowed by all the evangelists with a body different from the body they knew, with several new characteristics—difficulty of identification by the Magdalene and the pilgrims of Emmaus, instantaneous apparition, freedom from the general laws of matter and the like—which call to mind a glorified body. And is glorification not, precisely, the fruit of ascension?

Why, then, the forty-day delay proposed in Acts? Two avenues of research are open to us. The first consists in drawing up the list of references to the number forty in the Bible, and attempting to infer an adequate significance for this passage. One thing is certain, in any case. The number cannot pretend to calendar accuracy. Luke himself denies this, if we may say so, in referring later to the "many days" ($\epsilon\pi\iota$ $\eta\mu\epsilon\rho\alpha s$ $\pi\lambda\epsilon\iota\text{ov}s$) during which apparition had occurred (Acts 13:31). This is an indication that the chronological notation of forty days is not to be taken literally, as have done some of the "harmonizing" manuscripts in reference to Acts 10:41.

The Bible furnishes several examples of the symbolism of this number, but it will suffice to glean a few characteristic instances. It took forty days for the waters of the Flood to subside (Genesis 7:4). Moses remained at the summit of Sinai throughout forty days (Exodus 24:18), a reduced model of the forty-year pilgrimage of the people through the desert before entering the Promised Land (Numbers 14:34). This trek through, or sojourn in, the desert took place over a period of time thought to be considerable on the scale of a human lifetime. Elijah (1 Kings 19:8) and Jesus himself (Mark 1:13 and parallels) made similar forty-day sojourns in the desert before inaugurating their public ministry. In brief, the number forty has a conventional value, representing a time of preparation, its duration variable but unknown. Forty days, or forty years, are the sign of a salutary event about to occur.

A second direction cannot be neglected, though it is less traditional. The reference to a six-week interval is the only element literally foreign to the account of the Ascension as such. These weeks mark the period during which Christ appeared to his apostles. They do not necessarily imply that the Ascension occurred at the very end of that time. Moreover, the forty days are mentioned in verse 3, while in verse 2 reference is made in the past tense to the completed paschal mystery. Nothing, in summary, indicates that Luke intended to assign the Ascension event specifically to the fortieth day after Easter.

Other arguments as well favor this interpretation of the event. The notion that Jesus' ascent does not depend upon the end of the apparitions appears as well in Paul's works, when he enumerates, as a guarantee of the truth of the Resurrection, the official list of apparitions: ". . . he appeared to Cephas, after that to the Eleven . . . .³ Then he was seen by more than five hundred brethren at one time. . . . After that . . . by James, then by all the Apostles. And last of all, as by one born out of due time, he was seen also by me" (1 Corinthians 15:5-8). All these apparitions, including the one Paul received on the Damascus road, are placed on an equal footing. And no one would hold it necessary to postpone the Lord's Ascension until after this account of conversion.

The refusal to place any link between the notation of forty days and the Ascension itself still does not explain the role of this period in the account. To do so we must recall the similar period Luke had mentioned in reference to Jesus at the outset of the Gospel. That forty-day period had obviously been a time of preparation for the ministry awaiting the Lord. Reasoning **a pari,** and considering the Church as Jesus continued, we could say that the forty days in Acts constitute a period of preparation of the Church for its ministry. The remark has been made that forty is, in the East, a cycle number. In Israel especially, since Moses remained forty days in colloquy with God on Sinai, the number had become significative of divine revelation. The rabbis, it is said, had the custom of repeating forty times their instructions to their pupils, "in order that they might learn them by heart and in their turn pass them on in their totality and without alteration."[4] It is undeniable that such an interpretation fits perfectly into the cadre of Acts 1:3-8 wherein the theme of teaching by the Risen Master plays so great a role.

b. Mount Olivet. Like the moment, the locale of the Ascension is mentioned only in this account. It is near the place referred to in the third Gospel, Bethany, but cannot be identified with it. In spite of the lack of attention given to the theological aspect of Luke's geography—recalling that it was for doctrinal reasons that he chose to ignore the Galilean apparitions and—to make Jerusalem the pivotal point of these two books—one may legitimately question the choice of Mount Olivet as the point of departure for Jesus' return to his Father.

To situate such an event as this upon a mountaintop is quite biblical. For the man "of the Bible" the mountain is indeed a theological rather than a topographical reality. He realizes that a mountain once played a determining role in his history. It was upon the mountain of Sinai that the prodigious encounter of God with man was effected. At that very moment Israel was born as God's people, God's child. The recollection of such places had always remained strong in memories and in traditions. These were indeed privileged places. The prestigious locale which had witnessed the encounter of God and man comprised, upon reflection, two complementary notions. On the other hand, God had manifested himself in that place, and there he had concluded a covenant with his people. Thus the mountain became the place of election for the man seeking contact with God, the place of predilection for God seeking to reveal himself to man.

The religious person felt called to repeat this extraordinary experience. It was possible for few to return to the Sinai of the Exodus; for most who wished to make the long pilgrimage it was impossible. No matter! If men could not return to the Holy Mountain, why could God not come to hallow the mountains of the Promised Land? Spontaneously, men sought to meet God upon the summits they saw, in any event, as the ladder and the footstool of the God of Heaven. On the one hand, they noticed that far from the noise of the valleys filled with human bustling the faithful could approach their God. On the other, if God should grant the grace of revealing himself, a man might receive from him a word of alliance, a revelation, a life-giving contact. He would have touched something of God's glory. For these reasons it was inevitable that men would choose mountains and hills upon which to erect terrestrial dwelling places for the divinity. Mount Zion in Jerusalem, Gerizim of the Samaritans, even the lowliest of altars tainted with paganism but still called "the High Place" answer to these sentiments. Thus the Palestinian highlands became Sinai in miniature.

It was perfectly natural then for Luke to situate this divine event upon a mountain. This motive alone would suffice to explain his geography, had he not been as precise as to name the mountain. Why, exactly, did he choose Olivet?

To answer that Luke, intending absolutely to center his account upon Jerusalem, merely accommodated his account to the only neighboring peak, Olivet, is indulging in trivia. The question must be examined more fully, and in this aim the most fertile source of information is the Old Testament. The Bible deals stintingly with the Mount of Olives. Besides the episode in 2 Samuel 15:30-32, which mentions the presence of a sanctuary at its summit, and a still vaguer reference in 1 Kings 11:7, which has no bearing on this matter, the Bible speaks only twice of Olivet, but both passages merit our further examination.

The former is found in Ezekiel, chapters 10 and 11. In this long vision Ezekiel witnesses the departure of the glory of Yahweh, which first leaves the Temple by the eastern gate (Ezekiel 10:18-22), then abandons Jerusalem to go and dwell upon the mountain east of the city (και εστη επι του ορους ο ην απεναντι της πολεως, 11:23), i.e., Olivet. In the meanwhile, the Spirit has possessed Ezekiel, dictating prophetic sayings to him and eventually taking him off to Babylon among the exiles (11:1, 5, 24) to whom the promise is made of the gift of a new Spirit (11:19— this summary glosses over long commentaries). When the glory of Yahweh leaves the earth, it is from Olivet that it takes flight, upon the cherubim, its usual vehicle in this context. Just as quickly, the prophet finds himself anew in the Spirit of God

($\varepsilon \nu \ \pi \nu \varepsilon \upsilon \mu \alpha \tau \iota \ \theta \varepsilon o \upsilon$), ready to bear his message: a new Spirit will be sent.

Parallel to this vision, and complementary to it is the one in Zechariah which occurs at the end of time. At that moment God returns for the final judgment and the glorious proclamation of universal Lordship: "That day his feet shall rest upon the Mount of Olives which is opposite Jerusalem to the East" (Zechariah 14:4). These descriptions are obviously complementary. The Mount of Olives is truly the footstool of the God of glory whenever he takes leave of the earth of men or makes contact with them.

Luke, had he intended, could not have made a more excellent or erudite choice than this to evoke the glory of the Risen One as he leaves the site of his Incarnation. By situating the event here, Luke implies that Jesus is the equal of the divine glory spoken of by Ezekiel. To be sure we are not misled, he lends to the angels who interpret this mystery a speech reminiscent of Zechariah. Is he not to return in the same manner, in glory, at the end of time, for the final judgment?

Luke's teaching is not limited to this analogy. The topographical detail, by recalling Ezekiel's vision, simultaneously reveals the profound significance of the Ascension. The reference to the gift of the Spirit also becomes obvious. Placing ourselves in the same situation as the ancient prophet and seer, we realize that the apostles are to be seized by the Spirit of God and sent out into the captive world to whom, in

their turn, they will bring the promise of a new
Spirit.

c. The Cloud. In an agricultural country, clouds
are too concrete a reality not to play an important
role in the symbolic expression of thought, particularly
of religious thought. Whether light and airy or dark
and menacing, clouds contribute to two types of
description. Ornaments of the heavens wherein God
dwells, clouds serve as chariots or steeds for his divine
journeys (Psalm 104:3). From the midst of heavy
storm-clouds thunders the voice of Yahweh. On the
other hand, white fluffy clouds' veil from men's eyes
the dwelling place of the Most High (Psalm 18:12),
protecting their gaze from the glorious brilliance of
the divinity. Gradually the clouds come to evoke the
glory of Yahweh, which they conceal.

This is their essential function in the pages of
Exodus, where the cloud, sometimes synonymous with
the Angel of God (Exodus 14:19), is unceasingly
present. In the form of a column it guides the people
in their wanderings. At the peak of Sinai, it veils the
all-pure glory of Yahweh (Exodus 16:10; 24:14-18).
It stands wherever God dwells, not only in the heights
of the heavens but also in the tabernacles of earth,
the Tent of Reunion (Exodus 33:9-10) and later the
Temple of Solomon (1 Kings 8:10). It would be fruitless to pursue this theme throughout the length of
biblical tradition. One can guess the necessary
presence of the cloud at the moment of the departure
of the glory of Yahweh from Jerusalem in the vision
of Ezekiel previously referred to (Ezekiel 10:3-4), just

as one can expect it on the day of the glorious return (Daniel 7:13; 2 Maccabees 2:8).

It was inevitable that this image be used again in the New Testament to refer to Christ's glory. The description of a cloud accompanying Christ or hiding him from view is tantamount to a proclamation of his divinity equal to that of Yahweh. Because this divinity—a word synonymous with "glory"—is only made manifest after the Resurrection, there are few mentions of such a cloud in the Gospels. It appears only in the account of the Transfiguration when, for a moment, the glory of the incarnate Son is unveiled (Mark 9:7 and parallels). Its role is mainly eschatological, expressing the absolute glory in which the Lord will return for the final judgment (Matthew 26:64 and parallels; 1 Thessalonians 4:17; Apocalypse 1:7; 10:1; 14:4; etc.).

The cloud mentioned in this text must be interpreted as a witness to the total glorification of Jesus, and as a prelude to his return "in the same manner." The presence of this cloud is sufficient for the reader familiar with the Old Testament to herald the entry into glory of the Lord in the mystery of the Father.

d. The Angels and Their Disclosure. The angelology of the New Testament is linked without apparent hiatus with that of the Old, which had undergone a long evolution. Angels had been mentioned in the earliest books of the Bible, but it was particularly during the Exile that the science of celestial beings, enriched by contact with Persian angelology, became perfected, developed, and stabilized. Here we shall discuss only those notions helpful toward the understanding of this pericope.

In the beginning Israel distinguished only two sorts of celestial beings. The former were usually winged, and played an exclusively celestial role. They included the cherubim, seraphim, and other elohim, whose function was to praise and serve God, fanning him with their wings—an image borrowed from oriental court procedure. The latter are usually wingless, and serve as liaison between heaven and earth. Bearers of divine messages to the children of men, these are, properly speaking, the angels, i.e., "messengers." Their name is indicative of their function. Together the two constitute the celestial court.

Beginning during the Exile, angelology becomes more involved. Distinctions are made between good and evil angels. Angelic tasks become diversified, as, for instance, in the book of Tobit. Prophets and seers appeal to angels for the interpretation of their visions. Ezekiel, Daniel, and the Old Testament Apocrypha use them often to this end. In these writings the angel intervenes not merely to explain a difficult dream or vision, but also to guarantee the interpretation given to it. He is the infallible messenger of God. In this literary form the angel appears as a sort of **deus ex machina,** a literary device personifying the inspiration of the prophet. To further clarify this by an example, it might not be exaggerating to state that there is no fundamental distinction, i.e., none beyond that of literary form between the prophet proclaiming that he has received a message or the interpretation of an event directly from God (e.g., Jeremiah 1:11-12); the seer having an angel intervene to give him the significance of a vision (e.g., Daniel 8:15); and the theologian asserting that the interpretation and significance he gives an event are authentically divine. In the first two instances there is merely a question of the literary personification "word of God," "angel of God," of the unique theological reality, divine inspiration.

The New Testament proceeds similarly. It too mentions angel-servants of God, as those who intervene at the moment of the temptation in the desert (Matthew 4:11) or those who comfort the Lord in his agony (Luke 22:43). The angels who serve as liaison between heaven and earth are also mentioned, e.g., the angel of the Annunciation (Luke 1:26) and the one in the childhood account in Matthew (1:20; 2:13, 19). This second group also includes the angels who interpret the Resurrection (Luke 24:4) and the Ascension (Acts 1:10). These come in pairs, in order to guarantee by the double witness required by the law in serious matters (Deuteronomy 17:6) the truth of their message. They represent symbolically the real and effective although invisible assistance of God through whom the apostles are given to understand in depth the mystery they are to preach.

This message is short and simple, announcing the fulfillment of Christ's great pilgrimage ($\pi o \rho \varepsilon v o \mu \varepsilon v o v$). He has finally attained the Temple in heaven ($o v \rho a v o s$, repeated three times). This moment of the Lord's

life is last merely in appearance, for it is the prelude
and the guarantee of his return in the same mysterious
manner. The entire episode has an eschatological
bearing. Henceforth we live in the hope of his return.

e. The Eyewitness. There remains for discussion
one further original element, undobutedly one of
major importance, the eyewitness. In the several
sentences of this account, there are five references:
"Before their eyes . . ." (verse 9), Jesus is lifted "out
of their sight . . ." (verse 9); "They were gazing up to
heaven" (verse 10) when the angels asked why they
were "looking up" (verse 11), for this Jesus was to
come again as "they had seen him" going (verse 11).
Such an accumulation of references can hardly be
trivial. It is too unusual not to have a definite
purpose.

This purpose can be brought to light by an examination of that page of the Old Testament which
relates the assumption of Elijah (2 Kings 2:1:18). The
author insists first upon Elisha's desire to be present,
come what may, at the departure of his master (2:1-7).
Then, just before the decisive moment, there ensues
between the prophets the following dialogue:

"Elias said to Eliseus: Ask what thou wilt have
me do for thee before I be taken away from thee
[πριν η αναλεμφθηναι με απο σου]. And Eliseus said:
I beseech thee that in me may be thy double spirit.
And he answered: Thou hast asked a hard thing.
Nevertheless, **if thou see me** when I am taken from
thee [εαν ιδης με αναλαμβανομενον απο σου], thou
shalt have what thou hast asked; but if thou see me

not, thou shalt not have it" (2:9-10). When the fateful moment arrived, and Elijah "went up by a whirlwind into heaven [ανελημφθη Ηλιου εν συσεισμω ως εις το ουρανον]," Elisha saw (εωρα) (2:11-12). The end of this account draws the consequences of his vision. Elisha did in fact receive the spirit of Elijah his master, since he repeats immediately the same miraculous gestures as he. The prophetic brotherhood who were witnesses from afar to the scene understood this, and their submission to Elisha attests to the double portion of Elijah's spirit he had received. This "double portion" was the part of inheritance due the eldest son, successor to the head of the family, who enjoyed the same rights as he (Deuteronomy 21:17).

The text of the assumption of Elijah is obviously of major importance, as it makes brilliantly clear the significance of the Ascension as Luke presents it for our belief. He draws the explicit relation of cause to effect between the vision of Elijah's assumption and the gift of the double portion of the Spirit to Elisha. Luke here remains quite close to the Old Testament model. By the guarantee of the vision the apostles have just witnessed, we know that they will effectively receive the Spirit that Jesus has promised. The apostles are the Lord's spiritual heirs, to whom his message has been handed on, in whom it shall be continued. The elaborate setting and staging given by Luke in these several verses serve no other purpose than to confirm this.

3. **Conclusions**
   a. The Literary Form of the Account in Acts

1:9-12. At the end of this lengthy inquiry, the true literary form of this narrative becomes evident. Luke has deliberately undertaken a second account of the Ascension abounding in literary and theological artifices reminiscent of the Old Testament in order to confer upon this mystery a new significance which he was unable to express at the end of the Gospel. This second account was inevitable if he was to speak of the Ascension not only as the extension of the Resurrection but also as the prelude to the gift of Pentecost.

Such an account is derived from the literary form known as "midrash." Contrary to commonly accepted opinion, this term—derived from a Hebrew root meaning "to examine, to scrutinize" and applied especially to Scripture—has nothing to do with storytelling. It consists simply in a meticulous recourse to inspired texts in order to explain a religious doctrine difficult to set forth of itself because it would require too abstract a vocabulary. Such a literary form requires, obviously, that the constituent elements not be taken at face value. They are valid only in the significance with which they are charged, and which alone must be examined.

Luke was familiar with this procedure, having used it previously in the first two chapters of the Gospel. He had been dealing there with a mystery, the Incarnation, too profound to be expressed in less refined literary terms. Added to his concern here to compose at the beginning of Acts a literary pendant to his infancy Gospel was the same problem, to speak of ineffable mysteries. Who could fault him for having recourse again to the colorful procedure of midrash?

b. The Doctrine. In underscoring the significance of each element it presents, this account reveals its depth and its unity. It proposes to our faith a dual teaching. First, it clearly affirms the identity of the risen Jesus with the God of the Old Testament. Christ enjoys the same divine prerogatives as Yahweh. Henceforth he may no longer appear before our eyes unless he protects us with a veil of clouds, for the brilliance of his glory is as blinding in him as in the Father. He is in every respect the equal of that glory which had left the Temple in Jerusalem, and whose return was expected for the judgment of Israel and of the nations.

Also, a doctrine is given to complement the Gospel teaching that the Ascension is a moment of the total glorification of Jesus. The Ascension is also the prelude and the guarantee of the gift of the Spirit. The account given here is resolutely oriented toward Pentecost, which it announces and prepares. It also concerns the apostles. We see them now as the Lord's heirs, the receivers of his teachings and of his powers, the rightful bearers of his message. Their word may now resound to the ends of the earth and be received without mistrust, for it is truly the word dictated by the Spirit of Jesus.

c. The Historical Problem. There remains one final question, actually of secondary import, regarding the historical detail of this event. Is it possible to reconcile the data of Acts with those of the other works of the New Testament? It is, to be sure, but there is some divergence of opinion on the manner of that reconciliation.

For some, two distinct events are being described. While the Gospels situate, rightly, the total and definitive glorification of Jesus on Easter Day—i.e., in our language, within the mystery of the Resurrection—Acts would be concerned with an account of the vision of Jesus' departure, at the end of the series of apparitions granted the apostles. There is nothing, indeed, to constrain us to refuse Jesus' granting his followers such a consolation. There is nothing, either, to require us to admit it. First, such a distinction is unknown in the New Testament, and Paul's witness (1 Corinthians 15:5-8, analyzed above) tends to contradict this solution. Moreover, such vivisection of the mystery diminishes it considerably. For it is the unique paschal mystery which is at once the glorification of Jesus as well as the guarantee of the gift of the Spirit to the world.

A better knowledge of the literary form used here permits us to avoid this rather "concordistic" attitude. Why not simply admit that this is a literary doubling of a single act, required by the change in perspective, and the author's concern to furnish a complementary teaching? The case is not very different from the doublet worked out by Matthew and Mark in reference to the single multiplication of loaves. There is nothing here liable to shock a mind less curious for accessory detail than concerned with the message of salvation.

II

THE FORMATION OF THE
NASCENT CHURCH
(ACTS 1:13-26)

The Apostlic College and Its Entourage (1:13-14)

VERSE 13   *the upper room:* This is a room on the topmost story of a house. It is, properly speaking, a place for gatherings rather than a dwelling place. The word is proper to Acts (9:37, 39; 20:8). The presence of the definite article, in a strict sense, would suggest a place known to all. Attempts to situate this room, identified with the Cenacle, home of John Mark's mother (Acts 12:12), while not lacking in likelihood, are inconclusive. The general location, west of the city, enjoys the support of a serious tradition.

Peter and John: In reference to the listing of the apostles, see Note 3, below, pp. 65-69.

VERSE 14   *with one mind:* A very Lucan adverb, this word will be found in nine other instances in Acts, but it occurs only once in the remainder of the New Testament. It attests to the harmony of the primitive Christian community, expressing their communal spirit, their fellowship, of which their common dwelling place under one roof is an outward sign. Luke is often attentive to such discreet but intimate notations which revive the ambience of these early days.

steadfastly: Again this is a word dear to Luke (6 instances, vs. 4 in the remainder of the New Testament).

in prayer: Luke, a pious person, likes to insist upon the prayer of the early Christians, of which he is to give us some valuable examples (2:42; 3:1; 6:4; etc.).

with the women: The presence of these women— no definite article being used in Greek, they are quite nameless—raises the question of their identity. Some commentators, influenced no doubt by the curious reading in Manuscript D, which adds "and some children," have suggested the apostles' wives. It would perhaps be better to recall the group of women to whom Luke had paid benevolent attention in his Gospel (Luke 8:2-3). He is the only one to mention their names. In Acts, he will also refer to these "women of rank" who come to the aid of the missionaries (Acts 16:13-14; 17:4).

Mary: She alone is mentioned specifically by name, and her title "Mother of Jesus" is given. This is her final appearance in inspired writings. Her presence in this place at this time can hardly be fortuitous. It is required, so to speak, by the major role she had played in the childhood Gospel. At the moment of the Church's birth, this Body of Christ continued and lived, Mary must be mentioned and the title given which earns her this mention.

his brethren: Last to be named are the "brethren" of Jesus. They come after the women, almost as an afterthought. (The preposition "with" is repeated without grammatical reason in the best manuscripts of this text.) They, too, will not be mentioned again, despite the role some of them are to play in the life of the Church (James, mentioned by Paul in Galatians 1:19, and Jesus' brethren in general to whom he refers in 1 Corinthians 9:5). Might we be correct in our suspicion that Luke or the Church sought to keep secret their affiliation with the Lord? There are, indeed, some indications of mistrust with regard to them, the most pointed being, indubitably, the one in John 7:5: "For not even his brethren believed in him." If at the origin of the Church they sought to capitalize on their relationship to the Risen One, there is every indication they had little success. It will not be one of them who is chosen to Judas' place.

Note 3.   The Apostolic College

Luke gives here a list of apostles somewhat different from the one in his Gospel as to the order of names. It may be interesting to compare the four lists available to us. No historical conclusion could be drawn from such an examination, but even the simplest and most tenuous hypotheses have some interest.

The four lists are found respectively in Matthew 10:2-4; Mark 3:16-19; Luke 6:14-16; and Acts 1:13. The following diagram reproduces them. The sign + is equivalent to the Greek conjunction $\kappa\alpha\iota$ (and), which links names in the texts.

Matthew

I. Simon Peter +
   Andrew his brother +
   James of Zebedee +
   John his brother

II. Philip +
    Bartholomew
    Thomas +
    Matthew

III. James of Alpheus +
     Thaddeus
     Simon the Cananean +
     Judas

Mark

I. Simon Peter +
   James of Zebedee
   John his brother +
   Andrew +

II. Philip +
    Bartholomew +
    Matthew +
    Thomas +

III. James of Alpheus +
     Thaddeus +
     Simon the Cananean +
     Judas

Luke

I. Simon Peter +
   Andrew his brother +
   James +
   John +

II. Philip +
    Bartholomew +
    Matthew +
    Thomas +

III. James of Alpheus +
     Simon the Zealot +
     Jude of James +
     Judas

Acts

I. Peter +
   John +
   James +
   Andrew

II. Philip +
    Thomas
    Bartholomew +
    Matthew

III. James of Alpheus +
     Simon the Zealot +
     Jude of James

This table, we repeat, allows no more than conjecture. The list in Acts, last to be compiled, seems to divide the apostles into three groups of four. This seems to be the implication of the particular use of "and" here. The last group is diminished, obviously, by the loss of Judas. This impression is confirmed by a comparison with the other lists. While these do not use the same division, they have in common with Acts the same first, fifth, and ninth names (Simon Peter, Philip, and James of Alpheus), who seem to be group leaders. Let us review briefly the constitution of the three groups, numbered, for convenience, I, II, and III.

Simon Peter is always at the head of Group I, as expected. In all the lists this group is comprised of the two great families which each furnished two apostles. Matthew's list places Peter's family in prominence, Peter and Andrew preceding James and John. Might this be the former tax-gatherer's predilection for orderly arrangement? Luke here has probably copied Matthew, there being no reason for change. In Mark's list, though, James moves upward, coming immediately after Peter. John is mentioned in relation to his brother "John, the brother of James" as if the latter were the better known. Might it be that James's prominence comes after his martyrdom in A.D. 44 (Acts 12:2)? His place is all the more surprising in that Mark's links with Peter's family were surely closer than with the sons of Zebedee. Finally, the list in Acts changes the order again, John moving up into second place. In Acts 12:2, unlike the reference in Mark, it is James who is mentioned in relation to John, "James the brother of John." Obviously, John by this time had assumed the prior place. The memory of the martyred James has been diminished in favor of John, who may have been alive at the time Acts was written. In any event, if the earliest list is Matthew's, John's eminence seems to increase as time goes on. There is no practical point in referring to John's Gospel on the subject, as it gives no listing of the apostles. Moreover, we know that it never mentions Zebedee's sons. We must emphasize, however that in the Fourth Gospel, Simon Peter is most often mentioned of the apostles (22 instances), while his brother Andrew is referred to only six times. In all there are but six apostles named in John's entire Gospel.

Philip's name heads Group II on all the lists. Next to Peter's his is the name most frequently mentioned in John's accounts (12 instances), while the Synoptics merely include it in their lists. Is this a courtesy extended by the Metropolitan of Ephesus to his colleague, whose traditional see was neighboring Hierapolis, a city curiously omitted from the seven cities of the Apocalypse? It would seem, in any event, that Philip played an important role, completely unknown to us today, either within the group of Twelve or more probably, in the early Church. A like remark might be made concerning Thomas, whose prominence also seems to grow. If his accustomed place in this group was last (he loses it only in the first Gospel, as Matthew reserves it for himself), he is second to be named in Acts. This may be another indication of Johannine influence. The Fourth Gospel mentions him six times (vs. once in the Synoptics), and he is mentioned as a specially privileged witness to the Resurrection (John 20:24-29). This may be the reason for his increased renown.

It is not necessarily significant that Philip, alone among the apostles, has a Greek name, though it must be recalled that it was he whom the Greeks in John 12:20-21 had asked to serve as their spokesman to Jesus. There is still some way to go before this is considered sufficient indication of a Hellenistic tendency in Group II.

But for the stable position of James of Alpheus at the top of the list, Group III is that of the least known, the most controversial. We must resign ourselves to ignorance about these persons, with the notable exception of the traitor Judas. He has a well-defined position, and he did not usurp it. Despite the age-old controversies, it seems fairly well established that James of Alpheus, called the Lesser, is not James, brother of the Lord. Likewise Jude (son) of James,[6] whom Matthew and Mark know as Thaddeus, called "Judas, not the Iscariot" in John 14:22, is to be distinguished from Jude, the brother of the Lord mentioned in Mark 6:3. Finally, the same sort of confusion is to be avoided between Simon the Cananean, or Zealot, and Simon the brother of the Lord (Mark 6:3; Matthew 13:55). Still, it is remarkable that three of the four names in this final third of the list are identical with names of Jesus' brethren. Lastly, it adds nothing to point out that the Fourth Gospel does not mention these apostles, with the obvious exception of Iscariot, whose pitiable role gained him eight references.

The Replacement of Judas (1:15-26)

VERSE 15   *And:* The use of this conjunction (omitted in CCD) at the beginning of an account which bears no grammatical or logical relationship with the preceding context, while awkward and superfluous in our language, is common usage in Hebrew. The pericope relating the replacement of Judas deliberately imitates Hebrew usage, as in its preference for simple parataxis—the linking of disparate elements into a single sentence by the conjunction "and" rather than more precise copulae (cf. especially verses 18-19, 23, 26). This is an indication that the author has sought to give this passage an archaic flavor, resembling Old Testament narratives. For the exegete, it is also a sign that he must mull through the Old Testament seeking the key to the interpretation of this difficult passage. Notice that "in these days" which lacks any chronological definition and "stood up" are both deliberate and current Semitisms.

Peter: The initiative is his alone. This underscores his predominant role in the new community. The rest of this commentary will show how tradition has sought further to increase his importance.

brethren: The name by which the early Christians called one another. Previously they had called themselves "disciples," from their relationship with the Teacher who accompanied them. After the Lord had gone, they called themselves "brethren" in view of the relationship of charity uniting them.

persons: This is the meaning, in this instance of the Greek ονομα, a usage current in the language of the Septuagint (cf. Numbers 1:18, 20 and Apocalypse 3:4; 11:13).

meet together: This expression paraphrases the Greek επι το αυτο. Current in the Septuagint Psalter, this expression usually signifies "together" (as, for instance in Psalm 2:2 quoted in Acts 4:26). Elsewhere in the Old Testament it generally means "in all, totally." There is some hesitation as to which sense is preferable in this context. As the former is accepted in all other uses of this expression in Acts (2:1, 44, 47) and in Luke 17:35, it seems best to keep it here as well. It must be noted here that this text does not limit the number of Christians to 120. This number refers only to those present. Finally, the Hebrew equivalent is found repeatedly in the Qumran texts in reference to the unanimous community.

a hundred and twenty: This figure may be surprising in contrast to the handful of faithful mentioned in the previous verses. There is every reason to believe that a considerable time had elapsed between the two accounts. This will be brought up again in Note 4. According to their various personalities and preoccupations, commentators have given the most diverse explanations for this figure. Jurists have recalled that 120 is the minimum required by the law for the constitution of a smaller Sanhedrin, with jurisdiction over the internal affairs of a community. The election of a replacement to a vacant position would thus be valid and licit. Symbolists and mathematicians were quick to divide the number into its components 3 x 40. But despite Luke's predilection for the number forty and for artificial computations —especially in the childhood Gospels—it is difficult for us to draw any teaching from such a combination. Those historians are perhaps best advised who have recognized here an organization of a dozen "cells"— one for each apostle—of ten brethren, in imitation of the Qumran institution. It is not unlikely that the voluntary exiles of the desert of Judah indirectly influenced the organization of the primitive Christian community. Finally, there are those who think it rather probable, after all, that there merely happened to be at that time about 120 persons present. In any event, the figure is approximate: "about a hundred and twenty." To sum up, this information allows all sorts of hypotheses, but authorizes no definite conclusions.

VERSE 16   *Brethren:* Literally "men-brethren" according to Luke's style, as mentioned above (verse 11). We learn here, not surprisingly, that Peter is addressing himself exclusively to the male members of the community. The women will not participate in this election. Those referred to in verse 14 seem to have been forgotten.

The Scripture: In the singular, the word refers to a particular passage of the Old Testament, the plural "Scriptures" usually designating the inspired books as a whole. The fact that in verse 20 excerpts from two different psalms are quoted is insufficient to require the plural here. On the other hand, there is some reason for surprise at the space separating the texts from this introduction. This is a result of an unexpected excursus on the subject of Judas' death inserted here. This literary problem is to be discussed further in Note 4, below.

must be fulfilled: The manuscript tradition is divided here between the imperfect (which would read "had to be fulfilled" in English) and the present. If the latter be preferred it must be understood that the fulfillment of the Scripture bears on the necessity of replacing Judas. The imperfect, on the other hand, would suppose that the fact that Judas is dead—or more exactly, that he has deserted his post—fulfills the prophecy. The Scripture quoted below (verse 20) leaves open both hypotheses. The second is preferable, though, and not merely for philological reasons. The best manuscripts do use the imperfect, but there are theological reasons as well, as explained in Note 4, below.

the guide: οδηγος: an extremely rare word, reserved in the New Testament to the parable of the blind man who **guides** other blind men into a pit (Matthew 15:14; 23:16, 24; Romans 2:19). In the Old Testament it is used only five times. The most revealing use is in 2 Maccabees 5:15 where this noun describes Menelaus the traitor—the word used is προδοτης, used again by Luke in 6:16 to describe Judas—to laws and to nation. This double reference—to the person and to the book—is remarkable, and we shall come back to it shortly. Also remarkable is the fact that Luke shows an interest not evidenced by the other New

Testament writers in the deuterocanonical books of
the Old Testament, especially 2 and 3 Maccabees.
This interest increases, becoming more evident in
Acts than in the Gospel. Statisticians have numbered,
among the words proper to 2 and 3 Maccabees, only
two items used again in Matthew, none in Mark, nine
in Luke, and twenty-seven in Acts. Simple statistics
do not suffice for the drawing of any conclusions,
but it is no surprise that the two books which deal
with a particularly troubled period in the Church of
Israel have an interest for the historian—if he may be
called that—of the Church of Jesus Christ.

arrested: συλλαμβανω: a verb taken from the Passion accounts (Matthew 26:55; Mark 14:48; Luke
22:54; John 18:12). It is used frequently by Luke (11
instances out of 16 in the entire New Testament).

VERSE 17   *was allotted:* The verb derives from
λαγχανω, which usually connotes "to receive by lot"
or "to receive as a gift from the gods."

his share: κληρος signifies primarily a lot, either in
the abstract sense "the lot fell to . . ." or in the
concrete, an object used to cast lots, a die, pebble,
etc. By extension, the word also may designate that
which has been acquired by lot, a portion, an allot-
ment. All three senses are used by Luke in this
account, the third here, the others in verse 26. This
sort of play on words is a definite element of Luke's
style.

ministry: This word literally means "deaconship"
and connotes service. The apostle is first of all a

servant, and more precisely a "minister of the word" (Acts 6:4), to which he is totally submissive.

VERSE 18   *a field:* χωριον designates a field, a plot of land, as in John 4:5, but indicates, in a larger sense, an estate, as in Matthew 26:36, in reference to the "country place" of Gethsemane. It may include a dwelling.

the price of his iniquity: The Greek expression is liable to two translations, corresponding to two different notions. The literal translation, preferred here, is that which best agrees with the context. Another is possible, considering Luke's formula a Semitism. It would refer to a "price of iniquity," i.e., an unjust and iniquitous price, just as the reference in Luke 16:8 to the "steward of injustice" means simply an unjust steward. This sense is not required here, despite the Semitic flavor of the entire episode.

having swollen up:[7] Commentators are sharply divided as to the precise meaning of the word πρηνης. As it is used nowhere else in the New Testament it is difficult to ascertain its signification. Etymologically it may derive from a stem προ meaning "forward," which would give the adjective a general sense of "leaning" or "falling forward." This is the sense required in the only Old Testament passage in which this word is used, a description of the sinner's fate after death. "For he shall rend them and cast them down headlong that they shall be speechless" (Wisdom 4:19). This is also the proper sense in the uses of this word in the Apocrypha (3 Maccabees 5:43-50; 6:23).

It is the most usual choice of the translators of Acts, who are undoubtedly influenced by this confluence of evidence. As important as it is, this argument must not eclipse another hypothesis, according to which the stem would be derived from words meaning "to swell up, to become tumescent" (as in Numbers 5:21, 22, 27). From these verbs are derived the substantives πρησις and πρησμα, meaning "tumor, swelling, abscess" and the adjective πρηνης, to which the translation "swollen, tumescent" best applies, fitting in best with the context and with this description of Judas' sorry end.

burst asunder: This is a somewhat euphemistic translation of a verb which properly signifies "to burst apart noisily." The adjective from the same stem means "obscene," especially in reference to noises. The word is a biblical **hapax.** The use of such a term must have been costly to Luke, whose natural sense of decorum would have preferred another choice, had he not been constrained by imperious motives, about which we shall have more to say further on.

VERSE 19   *in their language:* A scholar's distraction? Luke seems to forget that Peter is addressing himself purportedly in Jerusalem to men expected to know the language. It probably indicates the use of a pre-existing document.

Hakeldama: A simple transliteration of the Aramaic **hakel,** "field," and **dama,** "blood."

VERSE 20   *Let his habitation:* This Scripture is taken from Psalm 69:25. In the Septuagint version he undoubtedly used, Luke read plurals. "Let their habitation be made desolate and let there be no inhabitant in their tents" (Psalm 69:25, LXX).[8] For purposes of his own, Luke changed the texts and eliminated the reference to tents, which did not fit the situation he was describing. Such liberty in dealing with the Old Testament is quite common in the New. It might be best to underscore immediately the fact that this quotation does not refer in any respect to Judas' death. It is not even stated that death is the reason the residence is uninhabited. The owner has merely disappeared, for whatever reasons.

And: This modest little conjunction raises its own series of problems. Apparently, in the view of modern commentators, it links the quotation just made with another from Psalm 109:8. In this instance, there is some reason to be surprised at the fact that two distinct Scripture quotations are announced by the one introductory phrase in verse 16. This is, if I am not mistaken, the one instance in the New Testament where two consecutive quotations are linked by a mere "and." This unusual and unexpected καὶ has raised many attempts, all superfluous, at the literary vivisection of this pericope. Actually, Luke did not quote Scripture with the punctiliousness of modern exegetes, and there is every reason to believe he considered these two verses as a single text from the Psalter. He behaves as if he had found the two joined already, constituting a single Scripture. The "and" is in fact a part of the verse about to be quoted.

let another: This is the second half of Psalm 109:8,

which also required emendation. Where the Septuagint had used the optative "May another take his office" (Psalm 109:8, CCD).[9] Luke substitutes the imperative "His ministry let another take," the better to justify Peter's initiative. In summary, the combined quotation tends to prove through Scripture that, an office and its functions having become vacant through the disappearance or desertion of its holder, a replacement is to be sought.

ministry: Literally, bishopric, i.e., supervision.

VERSE 21   *went in and out among us* (AV):[10] An attempt to render a literal translation of the Semitism used here by Luke.

VERSE 22   *he was taken up:* This expression is identical to the one in 1:2, 11. See the commentary on these verses.

witness: See above, pp. 24-25, in reference to 1:8.

VERSE 23   *They put forward:* The literal translation is used in English—in French the impersonal **on** was used—the subject being either the entire community in assembly or the Apostolic College. Anxious to place Peter's role in greater relief, some manuscripts have substituted the singular "he put forward." But the plural is preferable to a tendentious singular.

Joseph: This individual bears three names. The first, Joseph, is a Semitic proper name. The second, Bar-Sabbas, is an Aramaic surname meaning "Son of the Sabbath," indicating possibly that he was born on that day, but more probably that he observed the day of rest with particular piety. The latter interpretation tends to justify the third name, Justus, equivalent in Latin to the Greek Δικαιος, used in the language of the Septuagint to describe a just and pious man. Notwithstanding his piety and his linguistically charged cognomen, Joseph has no advantage over the discreet Matthias.

VERSE 24   *They prayed and said:* Augustine's Latin text read "**Et praedicatus dixit**" in the singular, further emphasizing Simon Peter's importance.

Lord: To whom is this prayer addressed, to the Father or to the glorified Christ? The adjective καρδιογνωστης, "who knowest the hearts of all," is unknown in the Old Testament but the notion expressed is familiar. Yahweh alone is to try the hearts and prove the reins (cf. Jeremiah 17:10; Sirach 42:18; etc.). In the New Testament, the word is to be found only here and in Acts 15:8 where it obviously refers to the Father. In postapostolic writings, however, its use is more general, and it applies also to the glorified Christ. Moreover, in Luke's theology the choice of apostles is an act of Christ, not of the Father. Finally, Luke shows throughout Acts that Christians address their prayers to Jesus, become Lord by his Resurrection (cf. Acts 7:59; 9:14; 14:23; 22:16). It is Jesus entered into the glory of heaven whom the community asks to choose the twelfth apostle, as he had previously ‘chosen the others.

VERSE 25   *place:* The twelfth apostle had, in the plan of Providence, a determined place in the apostolic ministry. He left it willingly to take another, also written into the work of redemption.

VERSE 26   *they . . . them:* To whom do these pronouns refer? To whom are the instruments called "lots" given, and who gives them? Those questions intrigued even the earliest copyists of this text, and some believed it necessary to clarify the situation by the following emendation: "Their lots were given." If we understand correctly, two short sticks or two pebbles were taken to designate the candidates. This correction is inadmissible because it oversimplifies the situation, though this might well be the sense of the phrase: sticks or pebbles representing Matthias and Joseph were given to those designated to oversee the election.

he was numbered: Etymologically, the verb $\sigma\upsilon\gamma\kappa\alpha\tau\alpha\psi\eta\phi\iota\zeta\omega$ means "to choose unanimously." The word is derived from the noun $\psi\eta\phi$os, "pebble," as this was the most common instrument used to express suffrage. A white pebble expressed approval (cf. Apocalypse 2:17), a black, rejection. This method of balloting is recalled in Acts 26:10. The noun $\psi\eta\phi\iota\omega\mu\alpha$ is used in the sense of "vote" (in the most democratic acceptance of the term) in 2 Maccabees 10:8 (cf. 1 Maccabees 4:59). Strictly interpreted, the word would indicate a free election in which all male members of the community of 120 expressed their choice. This interpretation of the event would give another sense to the pronouns "they . . . them" referred to above. It must be noted that in Acts 19:19, Luke uses a similar verb $\sigma\upsilon\nu\psi\eta\phi\iota\zeta\omega$ in the sense, quite proper in classical Greek, of "to count among, to add to." There is no evident nuance between these two verbs. The translation seeks to maintain the amphibology of the original.

Note 4. The Replacement of Judas

During the cursive reading of this text a number of problems have arisen, the discussion of which has been postponed. This Note will offer some resolutions for them. Five questions, in summary, may be posed. The first deals with the literary unity of the passage, whether the additions grafted onto it might not suggest a number of editorial emendations. A second question, historical in nature, is concerned with the divergence between the account of Judas' death in Acts and the one in the Gospel of Matthew. There is also a theological problem which ought not be neglected, as to why a replacement was sought for Judas. Finally, there are two lesser questions to be dealt with, concerning the moment when that decision was made and the manner in which that replacement was designated.

1. The Literary Problem: The Unity of the Text

A barely critical reading of the pericope relating the replacement of Judas will suffice for an appreciation of the literary difficulties involved. The edition has been disturbed to the point that commentators have suspected the intervention of one or several foreign hands who have reworked, more or less cleverly, a Lucan text originally much shorter. Is it really plausible that Peter spoke the discourse in verses 18-19 to residents of Jerusalem, who were in a position to be informed of the situation and whose native tongue was Aramaic? Moreover, this speech is an untoward interruption between the introduction of a Scripture (verse 16) and the text itself (verse 20), contrary to current usage. Again it would seem that two verses are referred to, but a single quotation was announced. Finally the conclusion drawn is based entirely upon the second element of the quotation.

This is the basis of a long-standing question. Might the former quotation be superimposed? The text would certainly flow better if verses 18-19, or even verses 16b-17, were eliminated. In this case, the Western Text for verse 16 "must be fulfilled" (present tense) would be preferable to the imperfect of the current Greek text. In other words, it may be possible to assign the offending verses to an interpolator.

The most extensive philological study does not allow an affirmative conclusion. As loosely knit as this account seems in its present state, it is written, even in the additional verses, in Luke's own style and vocabulary. One solution to the question of quotations has been suggested, that there is basically only a single citation, under one introduction, presented as an unbroken text. Luke may have had access to a Jerusalem tradition, perhaps already set in writing, concerning the replacement of Judas, which he reworked to make it intelligible to Theophilus. Moreover, he must have accommodated it to his own theology. The moment seemed opportune to make a discreet reference, in verses 17-18 of the present text, to Judas' death. Such a procedure seems approximately equivalent to our own system of footnotes.

The conclusion of the following section, concerning the historical problem of Judas' death, will show why Luke was concerned with the details interpolated here, and will demonstrate that Luke alone, or some disciple of his intimately familiar with his theology, could have made this addition.

2. The Historical Problem: Judas' Death

The twelfth apostle's end is related in two texts, this one and Matthew 27:3-10. The lack of similarity between them is too pronounced not to be remarkable. On the contrary, it must be emphasized, the better to justify their differences and to express their richness.

Each of these texts contains three elements: the circumstances of Judas' death, an explanation of the Field of Blood, and a recourse, implicit or explicit, to Scripture. We shall examine each of these elements.

First, the death of Judas. If we understand the text correctly, Acts describes a sickness causing swelling or tumefaction of the body ($\pi\rho\eta\nu\eta s$ $\gamma\epsilon\nu o\mu\epsilon\nu os$) as a result of which disembowelment caused rupture of the intestines. In Matthew the death is described by the single word $\alpha\pi\eta\gamma\xi\alpha\tau o$. The verb $\alpha\pi\alpha\gamma\chi\omega$ has as its first meaning "to squeeze, to crush" (cf. the English "anguish" and "strangle"). In the middle voice, the verb means "to strangle oneself," "to hang oneself." These meanings are classical and indisputable. It would be fruitless to attempt to harmonize the two accounts. The hypothesis of a rope which broke, causing the hanged man to fall forward head first (πρηνης), breaking open his abdomen, derives not from exegesis but from fiction.

Moreover, Matthew situates the hanging of the traitor on the morning of Good Friday, following a spectacular gesture in front of the high priests—whom the immediate context describes as gathered in a different place debating the death of Jesus (Matthew 27:1, 12). Luke, on his part, furnishes no chronological detail, but the very illness with which he afflicts Judas would suppose the passage of a considerable length of time.

The question of the Field of Blood is hardly clearer. Luke relates that it refers to a small property (χωριον) bought by Judas himself with the proceeds of his misdeed. Later, it seems, the spot became known as the Field of Blood because Judas' own blood was spilled there. Nothing suggested that the traitor felt remorse. Matthew, on the other hand, shows a contrite Judas (μεταμεληθεις) who brings his thirty coins back to the priests and, faced with their refusal to accept them, throws them dramatically at their feet. It is the high priests themselves who then acquire a plot of land (αγρος) which the evangelist specifically mentions as having belonged to a potter. This plot was given over to the burial of foreigners and soon became known as Hakeldama because it had been purchased with the price of Jesus' blood. The only element common to both accounts is the toponym "Field of Blood," and it is differently explained in the two texts.

The problem of the Scripture quotations is still

further embroiled. Formally, Luke uses no Scripture passage to explain Judas' death. His references are directed, rather, toward the question of replacement. At best, one might consider the use of Psalm 69:25 an interpretation of Judas as a persecutor and detractor of the suffering Just Man, as this is the context of that psalm. However, it is not certain whether the reference was chosen with this context in mind, or for its own sake. There is little to be drawn from the account in Acts in solution of the problem which preoccupies us presently.

Matthew claims to base himself upon a prophecy of Jeremiah: "Then what was spoken through Jeremias the prophet was fulfilled. And they took the thirty pieces of silver the price of him who was priced, upon whom the children of Israel set a price, and they gave them for the Potters' Field, as the Lord directed me" (Matthew 27:9). This long quotation is actually the result of an involved mosaic of texts. The basis is not Jeremiah, but Zechariah 11:12-13, a text previously used by Matthew in the preceding episode in which Judas had been involved (Matthew 26:15). "And I said to them 'If it seems good to you, give me my wages, but if not, let me go.' And they counted out [$\varepsilon\sigma\tau\eta\sigma\alpha\nu$, Matthew 26:15] my wages, thirty pieces of silver. But the Lord said to me 'Give it **to the Potter** the handsome price at which they valued me.' So I took the thirty pieces of silver and gave them **to the Potter** in the house of the Lord."[11] This seems to be the rather mysterious text the author of the first Gospel had found in his Hebrew Bible.

It is obviously difficult to determine what role a potter might have in this affair, and the presence of one in the Temple is, to say the least, unexpected. This is why a long tradition, antedating Matthew, had known a correction which, by the substitution of a single letter, eliminates the embarrassing potter (Hebrew: YWSR) replacing him with "the Treasury" (Hebrew: 'WSR), more appropriate in this context. Regardless of the value of this correction, which seems evident, Matthew either was unaware of it or else deliberately ignored it. In any case, the text from Zechariah does not seem to justify either the purchase of the field or its possession by a potter. By what roundabout way has Matthew come to combine these details with the prophecies?

He suggests the answer himself, and the commentators agree. It is through an imbroglio of recollections from Jeremiah. The false potter of Zechariah 11:13 must have reminded the evangelist of the contacts Jeremiah had had with the potters of Jerusalem (Jeremiah 18:1-12). The presence in Jerusalem of a field known as Hakeldama recalled the field Jeremiah had purchased at Anathoth at the Lord's command (Jeremiah 32). Here we are confronted with a most mystifying combination of texts from the Old Testament. But what conclusions may be drawn from all this?

A first conclusion concerns Judas' field. It is obvious that the combination of texts made by Matthew is much too subtle and complex to have been the basis for the Potter's Field tradition. This tradition undoubtedly predates the literary amalgam which sought, at a later date, to justify or support it by rabbinical procedures, for what they were worth. We can hold as certain that Jerusalem knew, when Matthew composed this text, a Hakeldama associated with the traitor Judas. It is also possible that this field had something to do with a potter. Since the fourth century of the current era, at least, this property has been located south of Jerusalem near the confluence of the valleys of Kedron and Ge-Hinnon, not far from the Potter's Gate. It has been rightly observed that this was the site of the industrial quarter of the Holy City, the location of the homes and shops of the founders, potters, drapers, etc. The link between this plot and Judas must have been sufficiently vague to permit explications as varied as those in Matthew and in Acts.

The second conclusion deals with Judas' death, and it is more interesting, though more hypothetical. As has been said, the link between Hakeldama and Judas Iscariot is obscure, uncertain, indicating that the circumstances surrounding the traitor's death were not well documented. It is also likely that he did not seek to increase his pitiable notoriety after the betrayal. Thus, the evangelist who wished to concern himself with Judas' end was free to write as he pleased, to keep primarily in mind his own didactic and theological aims. He could also make use as he pleased of the various bits of tradition bruited about. Better still, he might recall Old Testament examples in order to cast light upon the role of this

individual. It is not difficult, in fact, to rediscover
the models which inspired both Matthew and Acts.

Beyond the extraordinary and rather heroic instance of warriors falling upon their swords to escape
the enemy, Matthew knew that the Old Testament
related but a single case of suicide, and that by
hanging. It was thus that death came to Achitophel,
the traitor who had cunningly devised the fall of
David by selling out to Absalom. He had actually set
about to surpise David and his followers at the head
of a great army, at a moment when David's men
were lacking in strength and courage. He hoped they
would scatter without resistance and that he could
take his sovereign captive (2 Samuel 17:1-3; the
incident is not without parallels in the account of the
arrest of Jesus in Matthew 26:36-56). Absalom, however, refused in the end to follow this plan. "Achito-
phel . . . departed . . . and hanged himself" ($\alpha\pi\eta\lambda\theta\varepsilon\nu$
. . . $\kappa\alpha\iota\ \alpha\pi\eta\gamma\xi\alpha\tau o$, 2 Samuel 17:23). The phrase directly
recalls the Gospel account "and he [Judas] went
away and hanged himself" $\kappa\alpha\iota\ \alpha\pi\rho\eta\lambda\theta\omega\nu\ \alpha\pi\eta\gamma\xi\alpha\tau o$,
Matthew 27:5). Thus the evangelist declares his in-
tention, to depict Judas as the consummate traitor,
the renegade, the man who realizes pitiably the
prophecy of Achitophel. At the same time he suggests that Jesus is the new David, persecuted by his
own, affirming as well, indirectly, his effective king-
ship over Israel.

Luke's description in Acts orients us in a different
direction. The relationship between Jesus and Judas
was pertinent to the Gospel, but irrelevant in this

book of the Church, in which it has no place. The episode is now to be judged from the viewpoint of the Church.

The malady which causes Judas' death, as distasteful as it may be, is not without parallels in biblical tradition. In the Bible, a degrading death usually comprises the following characteristics: putrefaction of the flesh, gnawing of the remains by worms, bursting of the bowels, and nauseous odor. We owe to Luke's good taste and sense of decorum the fact that we are spared these literary details. He is inspired by such examples, having undoubtedly read the death of Antiochus Epiphanes in 2 Maccabees 9:5-10, and the similarly recounted demise of Herod the Great in Josephus' account (**Antiquities** 17, 168ff.). Luke will again use this procedure, but still more discreetly, in relating the death of Herod Agrippa (Acts 12:23).

The most important element to be noted here is that such a death is reserved not to traitors but to impious great men, especially to the persecutors of religion. It is the death of such as sought the destruction of the Church of Israel (Antiochus) or Jesus Christ (Agrippa and, in later Christian tradition, Julian the Apostate's contemporaries). The account of Judas' death is written to conform with the orientation of Acts. An occasion having been provided, Luke makes this insertion in order to witness that Judas, by his betrayal of Jesus—a fact founded upon church history—had persecuted the Church and had become the model of all future persecutors—a fact founded

upon the second book addressed to Theophilus. The
Church is indeed Jesus continued and lived.

We are now surprisingly well informed as to
Luke's ecclesiology. As has been said in reference to
the Ascension, it must be repeated here that discrepancies between the account in Acts and those
in the Gospels either cancel each other out or
explain each other, keeping in mind the perspective
proper to each book's specific subject: the Savior,
the Church.

3. The Theological Problem: The Replacement of Judas

One well might ask why the Eleven sought to
replace Judas. When James was martyred in A.D. 44
there is no evidence that the remaining apostles
sought to confer his place upon a successor, though
there was a candidate, and a quite able one, available
in the person of Paul. It is remarkable, too, that he
never claimed such a place, to which his call and
his ministry seemed to entitle him.

Actually, as shown in Luke's account, the problem
was not raised by Judas' death, to which Luke barely
grants a mention, a footnote, to bolster his general
ecclesiology. The bearing of this account and of the
Scripture quoted is less upon the physical death than
upon the desertion of one of the Twelve. It is the
defection which requires the replacement. There is
a marked insistence upon the role of Matthias, who
is to assume a function no longer assured by Judas.
He will take a place become vacant not by the fact

of death but by reason of betrayal, through which Judas had assumed a new function, a new role. When James is gone, no one will seek to replace him, for no one will imagine that his place has become vacant. With the defection of Judas, the Apostolic College had become the College of Eleven. Upon the death of James it remained the College of Twelve.

All this attests to a very exact appreciation of the eschatological role of the Twelve in the theology of the early Church. The Twelve are the instrument of the infallible transmission of the redeeming Good News throughout salvation history. As long as that history endures, the role of the Twelve, instituted by Christ, is not ended. It will not be ended until they take their places on the twelve heavenly thrones, and the judgment of Israel is pronounced. From this viewpoint, the Twelve form an order apart, which can never be replaced. They are not a moment in the Church's history, but its permanent foundation. "And the wall of the city has twelve foundation stones, and upon them twelve names of the Twelve Apostles of the Lamb" (Apocalypse 21:14). None can replace them, for their death is not a disappearance. To perpetuate their action upon the earth, men will succeed them, to whom they have granted some portion of their power and of their office.

4. The Chronological Problem: The Time of Judas' Replacement

Luke situates the election of Matthias between the Ascension and Pentecost. What does this scheduling mean in reference to the actual calendar? It is impossible to determine, for, as we have seen, the chronology of the forty days is artificial. We shall never learn when the last visible manifestation of the Risen One to the apostles occurred, and we must be equally resigned to ignorance of the date of the first apostolic preaching.

Some indications would lead us to believe that the decision to replace Judas was not made immediately. In all likelihood it was not until after his death, which, according to Luke, was not directly linked with the events of Holy Week. Elsewhere, we see the emergence of a relatively structured community, even of hierarchical organization. This community of 120 contrasts with the small number gathered after the Ascension and even, if the interpretation of Acts 2:1, below, is correct, with the same handful of Christians present at Pentecost. Finally, the decision to replace Judas supposes an effort of theological reflection by the Church and by the Twelve which could hardly have been a matter of several days. Jesus' silence during the apparitions narrated by Luke strengthens this likelihood.

Again, the date designated by Luke for this event is more theological than chronological. The important point, evidently, was to associate Matthias in the complete paschal mystery to which he is a witness. Though he has followed Jesus from the time of John's baptism to the time of the Ascension, it is nonetheless necessary that he partake of the sending of the Spirit, by which the paschal mystery was to be fulfilled.

5. The Juridical Problem: The Mode of Matthias' Election

In the cursive reading of the text it was said that there are some indications which would favor a democratic election in which each voter indicated the candidate of his choice. A strict interpretation of verse 26 would tend to suggest this. It is doubtful, however, that this was the procedure used. Theological motives prevail over expressions whose meanings would have to be forced in any event. The immediate context as well as Luke's general theology favor the hypothesis of a drawing of lots, the usual mode of determining God's will (cf. for instance 1 Samuel 23:9-12). It is quite clear, in fact, that the Twelve constitute an order set apart, distinct from all other apostles and missionaries. They have been freely chosen by Jesus, the choice having been made through the intervention of the Holy Spirit (Acts 1:2). If one of them has defected, what human agency could direct the replacement? The prayer formulated in this instance, addressed to the glorified Lord, shows clearly that the choice is left finally to Christ himself. It is from him that the Eleven hold all power and mission. It is from him as well that the Twelfth must receive them.

The absence of any ritual of tradition of powers is enlightening in this respect. When, later on, the Twelve seek to relieve themselves of some of their duties in order to be more free for their ministry, they will institute deacons upon whom they will lay their hands as a sign of dependence and of the partial communication of their privileges (Acts 6:6). There is nothing comparable here, though such a ceremony might be in order if the Eleven had of their own initiative freely designated a co-opted apostle.

Concretely, one might recall the use of an analogous procedure in the Old Testament known as Urim and Thummim (cf. Exodus 28:30). This was an event in which two pebbles or two short sticks of different colors or bearing inscriptions were placed in a box with an opening. The box was shaken and turned over, and the object which came out designated the lot. This mode of consulting Yahweh was current until David's reign, when it disappeared completely. It served only during the earliest years of the Church. No further mention is to be made of it.

III

THE BIRTH OF THE CHURCH
(ACTS 2:1-13)

Pentecost (2:1-13)

VERSE 1   *And:* See above, page 70, in reference to 1:15. This conjunction is to be repeated seven times within the first four verses.

as . . . to a close: Literally "at the time the day of Pentecost was completed, or finished," this expression is in obvious contradiction with the ensuing account, which mentions the early hour of the morning at which this event occurred—verse 15, "the third hour," viz. 9 A.M. A similar difficulty existed in reference to Luke 9:51 (commented above, pp. 39-42). In both instances the construction is **ad sensum** and not intended to be taken literally. In fact, it is not as much the time of the event which is drawing to a close as the time of preparation. Luke 1:57 had required a similar interpretation. The ambiguity of this construction is undoubtedly grounded upon Luke's imitation of the Septuagint, where this expression is found, notably in Jeremiah 25:12.

Pentecost: Literally "fiftieth," this is the Greek name of the Jewish festival called "Feast of Weeks" in Hebrew. In reference to these various names, to the manner of calculating the date of this festival, and to its significance, see Note 5, below.

all: Who was there? The 120 brethren numbered in 1:15? The twenty-old persons named in 1:13-14? The commentators are divided, but the arguments in favor of the second hypothesis seem the better founded. First, the Pentecost pericope is better linked from the literary viewpoint with the end of the Ascension account than with the episode of Matthias' election. Indeed, the same situations, described by the same expressions, are to be found in both accounts. The commentary to follow will underscore the points verses 1 and 2 of this pericope have in common with verses 14 and 13, respectively, of the previous chapter. Moreover, verse 7 will clearly state that all these men are Galileans, which is true of the small group of apostles and brethren of Jesus, and for the women, even if no mention is made of them; but who would surmise as much for all 120? Again, verse 14 mentions only Peter and the Eleven, which is to be expected, since the promise of the sending of the Spirit made at the outset of Acts (1:4-5) concerns only them. Besides, our study of the Matthias episode gave us the impression it was an addition, inserted there with some appropriateness but for strictly theological reasons. Luke had succeeded artfully in ending this account with the affiliation of the twelfth apostle to the College of Eleven, leaving in the shadows the scene and actors of the early part of his account. Having reconstituted the group of apostles, he is able to present, without awkward transitions and repetitions, the event of Pentecost which concerns them all. Beyond these literary motives, the theology of the Ascension account furnishes another weighty argument. The presentation Luke gave of that mystery made it, we have said, the final preparation for the coming of the Spirit, and gave the guarantee that the apostles were actually the Lord's heirs. The link between the two events is particularly close, and the Matthias account must be considered a necessary interruption.

together in one place: The union of hearts called forth by the former expression is made actual by their gathering in one place. In juxtaposition the two are not pleonastic at all; rather, they witness to the narrow bond among the bodies—and the souls. It is well to remark—as these comparisons will occur frequently—that at Sinai the people awaited the Decalogue and the Voice of the Covenant in the same Spirit, ομοθυμαδον, "with one accord" (Exodus 19:8). This same adverb is used in Acts 1:14 and some manuscripts insert it here.

VERSE 2   *suddenly:* Without preparation. This little word αφνω is proper to Acts (2:2; 16:26; 28:6).

from Heaven: This does not mean "from above" from a spatial viewpoint, but "divine" from the viewpoint of natural reality. We would undoubtedly say "supernatural." There is an evident comparison here with the voice at Jesus' baptism which "came from Heaven" (Luke 3:22) and, more generally, with the words of revelation (cf. John 12:29; Acts 11:9; Apocalypse 10:4; etc.). The expression was current in

the Old Testament, but special mention should be
made of its use in the description of the theophany
upon Sinai: "His voice was made audible from
Heaven . . ." (Deuteronomy 4:36). Behind the vocal
symbolism is hidden the reality of divine nature.

a sound: The Greek word ηχος is used to describe
a very loud, violent noise, whatever the source. The
only other use of the word in the New Testament is
in Hebrews 12:19, describing the sound of a trumpet.
Further along in this account Luke will refer simply
to a noise (φωνη, verse 6). Again this echoes the
biblical account of Sinai when the appearance of God
to Moses was accompanied by the sound (φωνη) of
thunder and the sound (φωνη) of trumpets which
resounded noisily (ηχει) according to the description
of Exodus 19:16.

as: A short word but very important in the vocabulary of Luke, who, more than any other New Testament writer, underscores the fact that we are dealing
with symbolism and imagery, not with literal description.

a violent wind: The sort of wind which accompan-
ies a major storm. There is some similarity between
this description and that of the storm during which
Paul was shipwrecked (Acts 27:40-41). The expression
is also reminiscent of Psalm 48:6 "Thou wilt break
the ships of Tarsis with a vehement wind."

blowing: The word reinforces the notion of a
whirlwind. It is as if hurricane winds had engulfed
the house.

it filled: The imagery is carried further to suggest the importance of the reality to be mentioned shortly. The wind which "fills" the house is preparing the coming of the Holy Spirit who, in verse 4, is to "fill" the apostles. The verbs in Greek are not identical, but based on the same stem, which suffices to allow the comparison. The literary technique is artistically perfect.

the . . . house: Inquisitive minds have not been able to refrain from the attempt to identify this house. Some commentators, impressed by the fact that Peter, without leaving, will shortly address a crowd of thousands, have taken the word in the cultic sense that it sometimes has and have concluded that the episode occurred in the Temple. There is nothing here to indicate this extension of the term, and the proposal errs by excess of historicism. Literary resemblances with the end of the Ascension account suggest instead the upper room referred to then (1:13).

whole: ολον: This detail is perhaps unimportant, superfluous, and irrelevant. On the other hand, it may be a studied reminiscence of Sinai, the mountain which "was **altogether** [ολον] on a smoke, because God had descended upon it" (Exodus 19:18).

they were sitting: The same periphrastic construction (ησαν καθημενοι) is used as in 1:13.

VERSE 3   *appeared:* The literal translation is "were seen," the passive being used because the phenomenon described here is supernatural. This mode of expression is current with Luke in describing apparitions

(Luke 1:11; 22:43; 24:34; Acts 7:2; 9:17; 16:9; 26:16). The divine reality is here called to mind by a new image, this time visual, adding further to the richness of aural symbolism of the previous verse.

distributing themselves:[12] The participle is in the present tense. The flames separate as they appear.

as of fire: Another watering down of the literary description, the flames are not fire, but like fire. A tongue of flame is a flame, nothing more—as in the expression "flames licking a log." Though the word "flame" is a part of Luke's vocabulary (Luke 16:24; Acts 7:30), to use it here would have meant the loss of an evocative play on words on the two senses of "tongue." Here we are made aware that the proper gift of the Spirit at Pentecost is apostolic, missionary zeal, represented here by the organ of speech, for speech is the source of faith (cf. Romans 10:17). Note, too, that fire is an essential element of the scene at Sinai (Exodus 19:18; 24:17).

settled: The verb is singular, but the last-stated subject, tongues as of fire, was plural. The common interpretation supplies the singular subject—one flame —considering this an awkward but intelligible construction **ad sensum,** a satisfactory but incomplete explanation. More likely, Luke kept this ambiguous turn of phrase, considering the actual subject of this verb to be not the image, flames, but the hidden reality, the Spirit, soon to be mentioned. This was understood by the Liturgy, which chants, "Seditque supra singulos eorum Spiritus Sanctus." The verb translated "settled" here literally means "sat," for the Hebrew vocabulary knew no other word for "to remain." The coming of the Spirit upon and within the apostles is neither occasional nor transistory but permanent, unlike the case of inspired men in the Old Testament. The Fourth Gospel also underscores the dwelling of the same Spirit with Jesus (John 1:32-33). Note, finally, that in the account of Jesus' baptism, the Spirit was compared to a dove coming down from heaven, an image suggesting implicitly the new creation by recalling the first creation, where the Spirit of God moved over the waters (Genesis 1:2). Here other imagery is used that no longer directs us toward the new creation, which has been related and accomplished, but to the promulgation of the law upon Sinai, that law which sealed the covenant between creature and Creator.

VERSE 4   *they were filled:* The verb is $\pi\iota\mu\pi\lambda\eta\mu\iota$, a very Lucan verb found in twenty-two instances in Luke-Acts, and in only two instances in the remainder of the New Testament. This is not the only time it has the Holy Spirit as its object. Luke had said the same of John the Baptist (Luke 1:15), Elizabeth (Luke 1:41), and Zachary (Luke 1:67), all examples from the childhood Gospel. This coincidence added to the one mentioned above confirms our basic thesis that this is truly the Gospel of the childhood of the Church.

to speak: The verb $\alpha\pi o\phi\theta\epsilon\gamma\gamma o\mu\alpha\iota$ is quite rare. It bears a connotation of solemnity. At the lowest stylistic level it would mean "to speak loudly and boldly." But this word belongs especially to cultic vocabulary. It is used when the reference is to "speaking oracles, judgments, proverbs." This is the sense used in Exodus 13:9, 19 and Micah 5:11. In the vocabulary of Acts, as we shall see in verse 11, the verb has as its object, implicitly or explicitly, the Good News of the Christian message, proclaimed in particularly solemn circumstances. This is definitely the case here, and the repetition of the verb in 2:14 confirms it. It is also the case in 26:25, when Paul proclaims his message before Festus. These references exhaust the uses of this verb in the New Testament.

different tongues:[13] In the most obvious sense, the reference is to languages other than their own, foreign languages. The meaning is the same as in the Sirach Prologue, verse 22 and close to that in Isaiah 28:11. The adjective "different" is again a word dear to Luke (8 instances in Matthew, 1 in Mark, 1 in John, but 32 in Luke and 17 in Acts). About the question of "speaking in tongues" see Note 6, below.

VERSE 5   *were staying:* It does not seem that all the people mentioned here could be merely pilgrims passing through Jerusalem during the celebration of the paschal feasts. This verb, repeated in verse 10, refers, rather, to men born in various parts of the empire but whose normal place of residence is now the Holy City.

Jerusalem: The city here has the role of a microcosm. Before the gospel is preached in all climes, it is to be preached to all nations gathered together in Jerusalem, as the prophets had foretold.

devout: This adjective, proper to Luke's vocabulary, refers to a religious quality, involving zeal but particularly piety, devotion, and fervor. Thus are described Simeon, the old man to whom the Spirit dictated the Nunc Dimittis (Luke 2:25) and the brethren who buried Stephen (Acts 8:2). Luke may be described as having a particular empathy for these men, perhaps due to his personal spiritual affinity with them.

every nation under heaven: This biblical expression describes, as in Colossians 1:23, the universality of mission. The commandment given in Luke 24:47 and repeated in Acts 1:8 is already being carried out through the Spirit.

VERSE 6   *were bewildered:* The verb συνχυννω is found only in Acts (4 instances).

VERSE 7   *were amazed:* From εξιστημι, "to be stupefied," this word is used by Luke to describe the reaction of the Temple doctors listening to Jesus who stayed behind among them (Luke 2:47). The initial Christian preaching elicits reactions similar to the first public manifestation of Jesus. It is a reaction we recognize as normal.

VERSE 9   *Parthians, . . .:* In reference to the various problems brought to light by this listing, see Note 7, below.

VERSE 11   *we have heard them:* The end of verse 11 and verse 12 repeat almost word for word verses 6 and 7. This is a literary clue that allows a con-

jecture that the list is merely parenthetical, inserted
artificially here, outside of its original context, causing
Luke to repeat himself.

the wonderful works of God: The expression is
known in the Old Testament, from which Luke has
borrowed it. These wonders ($\mu\epsilon\gamma\alpha\lambda\epsilon\iota\alpha$) are the object
of praise addressed to God by pious Jews who seek
to magnify ($\mu\epsilon\gamma\alpha\lambda\upsilon\nu\epsilon\iota\nu$) the Lord. What, exactly, are
these wonders? Often the works of creation, God's
creative activity, are called to mind (Sirach 17:8, 9,
13; 18:4; 42:21). No less often, the miraculous interventions of God in history during the Exodus are
remembered (Deuteronomy 4:2; Psalm 105:1; 106:21).
Generally, all the salutary manifestations of God on
behalf of men may be referred to (3 Maccabees 7:22).
These are the objects of Mary's praise in the Magnifi-
cat. These are also the referents in this text. The
apostles are publicly extolling the historical interventions of God, who has come to save his people and
the nations through Jesus his Son. Peter's entire discourse is an example of this sort of proclamation, a
summation of the Good News which contains the
ultimate **mirabilia Dei.**

VERSE 12   *perplexed:* From $\delta\iota\alpha\pi\sigma\rho\epsilon\omega$, "to be em-
barrassed, uncertain," this verb describes the state of
mind of one confronted with the miraculous, the
supernatural. The word is proper to Luke, who uses
it to describe Herod hesitating to believe the Baptist
has risen (Luke 9:7), the priests learning of the
miraculous freeing of the apostles (Acts 5:24), and

finally Peter himself following the dream which pre-
faces his mission to Cornelius (Acts 10:17).

in mockery: This reaction contrasts with the preceding, and it, too, represents an attitude. This is the
one use of the verb διαχλευαζω in the entire Bible.

Note 5.   Jewish Pentecost and Christian Pentecost

Luke, and he alone, chose as the setting for the
gift of the Spirit the Jewish festival of Pentecost. It
was not a random choice. Rather, it sought to give a
true and clear interpretation of the sense of the
Christian mystery which has, in a manner of speaking,
replaced and fulfilled the Jewish festival. It is important therefore that we recall the precise significance of this feast in the liturgy and spirituality of
Israel.

1. Pentecost in the Old Testament and in Judaism

The paschal feast dominates the Jewish calendar.
Its history and development are not clear but basically, it is the amalgamation of two very ancient pre-
Israelite festivals. The first is the Pasch, properly
speaking, a festival of nomads who celebrated it
every year just before the spring migrations. It con-
sisted primarily of offerings and sacrifices for the
welfare of the flocks. The second, the Feast of
Azymes (unleavened bread) was celebrated by seden-
tary farmers, who lived in Canaan long before the
Hebrews came to occupy the Promised Land. It
marked the beginning of spring and the start of the
harvest. Celebrated "when the sickle is first put to
the standing grain" of barley (Deuteronomy 16:9,

CCD),[14] it continued during an entire week. The chronological closeness of these two festivals brought about their fusion, the Feast of Azymes being celebrated on the second day of the Pasch.

The Pasch itself had by then lost practically all its significance, once the nomads had settled down. Moreover, like the Azymes, it was a pagan festival. A new significance was sought for the newly joined feasts, which was discovered spontaneously in the Exodus from Egypt. The great material and spiritual migration of the Hebrews had no doubt occurred at this season, the onset of spring (Numbers 33:3). This historical process helps to explain the more gradual development of the second pilgrim feast, that of Pentecost.

Initially this was also an agricultural feast, which closed the time of harvest and was celebrated at the end of the reaping of wheat (Exodus 23:16; 34:22). To fix its date more precisely, it was called the Feast of Weeks, as it occurred one full week of weeks (i.e., one more than seven times seven days, or fifty days) after the Feast of Azymes. Later on, for this reason, the reading assigned for this day was the scroll of Ruth, which recalls the double harvest of barley (2:17) and of wheat (2:23). Thus the harvest season was enclosed between two festivals, one which opened it (Pasch-Azymes) and one which closed it (Pentecost).

Pentecost long kept its status as a harvest festival. Its exact date was not fixed until quite late. First it

was necessary to stabilize the date of the Pasch, as
that of Pentecost depended upon it. The Pasch
eventually was celebrated on the night of the first full
moon of spring. Consequently, the Feast of Azymes
was held the next day. But various Judaic sects began
to hesitate, nonetheless, over the precise date of
Pentecost. At what point was the computation of the
fifty-day interval between these feasts to begin?
Calculations as subtle as they are varied were suggested, which are quite interesting. The Sadducees
considered the Pasch equivalent to a Sabbath, whatever day of the week it occurred, and fixed the date
of Pentecost fifty days later. For them this feast also
could be celebrated on any day of the week. The
Pharisees counted fifty days from the legal Sabbath
of the paschal octave. For them, Pentecost always
occurred on the day following a legal Sabbath, a
Sunday in our calendar. At Qumran, it was considered that the paschal celebration lasted eight days,
the entire octave to be counted as part of the feast.
They counted fifty days from the Sabbath following
the paschal octave. Thus, depending upon the various
systems of computation proposed, the interval between Pasch and Pentecost could be considerably
greater than the theoretical norm of fifty days.

As complex as they seem, these calculations and
computations—upon which agreement had not been
reached in Christ's time—have their usefulness. When
an attempt was made to give Pentecost a significance
commemorating the Exodus in conjunction with the
Pasch, the very flexibility of the fifty-day interval

allowed a coincidence with Exodus 19:1, a text
suggesting a sixty-day period between the departure
from Egypt and the arrival at Sinai. Despite the
different calculations, some agreement was reached,
just at the beginning of the current era, concerning
the historical significance of this festival, which became the commemoration of the promulgation of the
law on Sinai. Thus the Pasch-Azyme-Pentecost trilogy
constituted a liturgical unity, extending throughout
seven or eight weeks the central events of the
freedom-giving Exodus. It was precisely at this time
that the Sinai episode enjoyed, within Judaism, its
greatest period of commentary and reflection.

It is impossible to quote here the texts, or to fill
in all the developments contained in Jewish theology
on the subject beginning in the first century of the
current era. The basic notions which were discussed
at that time are summarized briefly insofar as they
concern the exegesis of Acts. Until recently, we have
had only the most doubtful sort of documentation in
regard to an identification in New Testament times
of the Pentecost festival with the commemoration of
the gift of the law to Moses. Rabbinical texts referring
to it date from somewhat later than the first century,
and the Book of Jubilees offers no real guarantees.
Translators are divided, in fact, on the meaning of
the word which describes the feast in this book. Is
it the Feast of Weeks or of Vows (both being accept-
able translations of the word in the plural)? The most
recent works on the subject favor the latter, going
against an identification of this feast with that of
Pentecost.

The Qumran documents, on the other hand, offer the hypothesis of a liturgical celebration of the gift of the law, the Sinai covenant, occurring on the day of Pentecost, at least in some Judaic sects. The Qumran community called themselves the Brotherhood of the Covenant, in fact, and it is known that Pentecost had a special significance among its members. It was on this day that the members of the Qumran community renewed their personal covenants, and that new brethren were admitted to the community.

If the Dead Sea scrolls attest to an identification of Pentecost with the gift of the law at the epoch which concerns us, they give no evidence with reference to the speculations made on the subject. Two other currents of thought, both known from other sources, must be consulted. Philo, a witness to the former of those currents, comments on the text of Exodus 20:18, which states literally that at the moment the law was promulgated the Hebrews "perceived the voice" of God. He explains that this was possible because that voice had taken the shape of a flame (**De Decal.** 46-49). Moreover, this divine voice, which was forming a covenant with his people and proposing it implicitly to all men, was audible to every individual, regardless of the distance separating him from Sinai, for all could hear it resound within themselves (**ibid.,** 33). This curious exegesis has echoes in rabbinic tradition.

The rabbis also knew the tradition of the voice-flame. They state that this voice was separated into

seventy dialects to allow the seventy nations of the
world counted in Genesis 10 to understand it. We
can easily guess the aspect of this which is to be
drawn into an interpretation of Luke's account. We
must also underscore the significance of the notion
of "church" in this context. The day of the gift of
the law was rightly considered the day of the birth
of the Church, the "day of assembly" (cf. Deuteronomy 4:10; 9:10). It is truly at this moment that
the "assembly," the εκκλησια, was constituted in the
unison of hearts and souls underscored in Exodus 19:8.

These few indications will suffice better to understand the design of this background against which
Luke's account is to be drawn. We may now briefly
summarize the essential elements of the doctrine he
has fashioned upon it.

2. Christian Pentecost according to Acts 2

In situating the gift of the Spirit on the fiftieth
day after Easter, Luke assures even more than is
initially evident the fundamental unity of the paschal
mystery, Easter-Ascension-gift of the Spirit. This
unity had not escaped the other New Testament
writers, who had merely expressed it otherwise. Thus
the Fourth Gospel seems to fit into the same theological tradition. For John, too, the two aspects of
Christ's glorification, the Resurrection and the exaltation at the Father's side, are considered inseparable
not only from one another but from the gift of the
Spirit, which is the purpose of that exaltation. Henceforth the evangelist merely has to discover a way of
expressing this profound unity. He achieves it by

bringing into the chronological unity of Easter day
the triple and unique mystery of salvation—Resurrection (20:8-9), Ascension (20:17), and mission of the
Spirit (20:22).

This arrangement could hardly have been adequate for Luke, as he was planning a book concerning the Church. Rather than a theological schema, he
prefers a liturgical schema, as it is in the liturgy that
the Church "recalls" the acts of salvation, commemorating and celebrating them. Now the liturgy, by its
very nature, requires some separation into various
aspects of the unique salvation event, a chronological
division for purposes of celebration. Again, if Luke
differs from the other New Testament authors by his
unique presentation of the paschal mystery, it is in
view of the unique orientation of his book.

Moreover, the parallel thus suggested between
the Christian Pentecost and the Jewish Pentecost
considered as a memorial of the Sinai covenant is
rich in doctrinal evocations, and it enlightened considerably the decisive event. Two aspects are particularly outstanding.

First, in the perspective of the salvific act, we
understand that the Christian Pentecost comes to
fulfill the Lord's Pasch just as the Sinai Pentecost
had fulfilled the Pasch of the Red Sea. In the image
and in the reality, the Pasch is the moment of freedom, liberating the Hebrews—or the new Israel—
from slavery and sending them out on the pathways
of the Exodus. Pentecost adds nothing to this free-

dom, which is complete, but comes to grant a way of living-out in the Exodus this status of free man, of saved man, which the Passing has given. This is the purpose of the law of Sinai, which gives the people the knowledge of the means whereby they may live as redeemed men, means which will be the measure of their faithfulness to the Passing. The same may be said of the Christian Pasch and of the Pentecost which fulfills it. The latter does not free mankind from the slavery of sin, for this freedom has been achieved totally in the Lord's Resurrection. It offers the means of living as risen men, a means which can no longer be **the** law, or any law, but which is the real Spirit of the glorified Lord. To live as risen man, it is enough to have within oneself the Spirit of the risen Jesus. The letter which killed is itself dead, but the Spirit gives life. The law had stifled—as experience had shown—but the Spirit is the source of the supreme freedom which is the heritage of the saved. The complete Pauline theology of the epistles to the Romans and to the Galatians subtends this page of Acts. Might it be possible that Luke, companion of Paul's missionary journeys, had them in mind as he wrote?

Second, from the perspective of the redeemed, Pentecost attests and gives substance to the constitution of the saved into an assembly. With the reception of the Spirit they are formed into a Church just as the Hebrews had been constituted into the People of God at the foot of Sinai, from whose heights the law had been brought to seal their union. The

Christian Church is the community of the risen, bound together into one heart and soul by their participation in the same divine Spirit—his intervention bears all the marks of a theophany—who acts in men by his power, his inspiration, and his gifts. He is to be, in and through the Church, the first weakness to the work of redemption, accomplished by the Son. The missionary endeavor of the Church, tabernacle of the Spirit, is brought to light at once by the "miracle of tongues."

Note 6. The Miracle of Tongues

The miracle of tongues on Pentecost has always caused curiosity and perplexity. Commentators disagree on its nature if not on its significance. They are separated by a dilemma. Was this a miracle of speech or one of hearing? In the latter hypothesis the listeners heard in their own tongue the words of the apostles, who were speaking either in Aramaic or in an inspired language normally unintelligible to human ears. In the latter case, there would be a double miracle, of hearing and understanding on the listeners' part, of speaking by the apostles. This phenomenon, a charisma rather than a miracle, is called "glossolalia." In the former instance, the apostles would have been granted the ability to speak without having learned, then, all the languages and dialects of the people gathered in Jerusalem. This particular charism is sometimes called "xenoglossia."

We hasten to mention: to state the problem thus is to state it badly. It directs our attention to what happened rather than to what Luke was trying to teach. What is important is Luke's teaching, which will offer some opportunity to learn more about secondary details. It will be necessary to review the various passages of the New Testament dealing with similar miracles and to compare them with this account if we are to draw any conclusions.

1. Parallel Passages

Three texts draw our attention. First, Acts 10:44-47. These verses follow the great missionary discourse Peter addressed to the centurion Cornelius. The speech is hardly completed when the Holy Spirit possesses the pagan listeners to the Word, for whose benefit the Pentecost of the apostles is renewed (verse 44). The first result is the amazement ($\varepsilon \xi \varepsilon \sigma \tau \eta \sigma \alpha \nu$) of the Judeo-Christians at the fact that these pagans also ($\kappa \alpha \iota$) had received the Spirit (verse 45). Immediately Cornelius and his companions begin to speak in tongues and to magnify God ($\alpha \nu \tau \omega \nu$ $\lambda \alpha \lambda o \nu \nu \tau \omega \nu$ $\gamma \lambda \omega \sigma \sigma \alpha \iota s$ $\kappa \alpha \iota$ $\mu \varepsilon \gamma \alpha \lambda \nu \nu o \nu \tau \omega \nu$ $\tau o \nu$ $\theta \varepsilon o \nu$, verse 46). This leads Peter to conclude that this Pentecost is identical to that which he and the other apostles had been granted (ωs $\kappa \alpha \iota$ $\eta \mu \varepsilon \iota s$, verse 47). There are three remarkable elements here. First is the obvious identity between these phenomena and those experienced by the Twelve. Second is the fact that the text does not state that the words spoken by Cornelius were understood. They were simply heard. Third, the nature of the charism is described as "speaking in tongues **and** magnifying God." What signification is to be given to that "and"? It may be explanatory (epexegetical καὶ), meaning "speaking in tongues, they magnified God." But it may be an ordinary coordinating conjunction, in which case two distinct actions are referred to: "they spoke in tongues, then they magnified [μεγαλυννειν] God." Here the proclamation of the wonder (μεγαλεια) of God is easily recognized. A comparison with the other passages tends toward the second sense, as we shall shortly see.

The next text is found in Acts 19:6. Paul imposes his hands upon the disciples of the Baptist at Ephesus (who had been rebaptized in the name of Jesus Christ), confirming them in the Spirit, of whom they had never heard. They begin at once to speak in tongues. Here again the gift is double, for once the Spirit possesses them, John's followers begin "to speak in tongues and to prophecy" (ελανουν τε γλωσσαις και επροφητευον). As in the previous text, there is a distinction—and this time a very clear one— between the two gifts, charismatic speech and prophecy. Understood in its wider sense, the latter is nothing but the proclamation of God's wonders mentioned in the other texts.

1 Corinthians 12-14 contains a long Pauline dissertation on the charisms with which the Spirit fills the Church. Paul forcefully asserts his doctrine on the subject, the essential points of which follow. If there are many actual charisms, they are all the work of the one Spirit. In his list, Paul clearly distinguishes between the gift of prophecy (προφητεια) and the gift of tongues (γενη γλωσσων) naturally coupled with that of interpreting tongue (ερμηνεια γλωσσων) (12:4-11).

A bit further on (12:27-30), Paul again takes up the distinctions between prophecy, the gift of tongues, and the gift of interpreting tongues. It is recalled a third time, emphatically, in 14:26-33, 39, where the apostle asserts the superiority of prophecy, intelligible and useful to everyone, over the gift of tongues which requires an interpreter. Finally, the text of 14:1-25 allows the conclusion to be drawn that the gift of tongues was fairly common to the early churches. These mysterious tongues were incomprehensible to the listener and required an inspired interpreter. In this charismatic speech the possessed man did not speak to others, but to God. The only effect on the listeners is that they think the speaker is insane ($\mu\alpha\iota\nu\epsilon\sigma\theta\epsilon$, verse 23). Obviously, Paul has no great sympathy for this sort of extravagant speech.

Finally, it will suffice merely to mention Mark 16:17, as no conclusion may be drawn from this text. Recalling the signs which will accompany the apostles in their work in the Church—all but one miracle is fulfilled in the various episodes of Acts—the conclusion of this Gospel simply states "they shall speak in [new] tongues ($\gamma\lambda\omega\sigma\sigma\alpha\iota\varsigma\ \lambda\alpha\lambda\eta\sigma\sigma\upsilon\sigma\iota\nu\ [\kappa\alpha\iota\nu\alpha\iota\varsigma]$)." Though missing from some versions, the adjective "new" is to be retained. It is doubtful however that this term offers much toward the interpretation of the problem.

In conclusion, all of the texts reviewed here describe a gift of tongues corresponding to glossolalia, a phenomenon having nothing to do with the miracle of speaking in foreign languages (xenoglossia), which

is never mentioned, but which consists in the proclamation of ecstatic, incomprehensible discourses. For
this reason, it is far inferior in dignity to the charism
of "prophecy," as the latter is intelligible and edifying
to the listener. It is reasonable to understand this
prophecy as the proclamation of the wondrous works
of God **mirabilia Dei.**

2. The Gift of Tongues in the Pentecost Account

The comparison of the foregoing observations with
the Pentecost account makes obvious a number of
divergences and a number of similarities. The most
evident similarity is the reaction on the part of all or
some of Peter's audience and on the part of the
Corinthians. Paul had said that persons unaware of
the situation would call those who spoke in tongues
mad (1 Corinthians 14:23). In the Pentecost account,
a part of the crowd takes the apostles for drunk,
which is hardly more flattering. On the other hand,
there are three clear divergences. First, the manner
of expression is somewhat altered. In Acts the reference is not merely to "speaking in tongues"—the
expression used in both singular and plural in the
other texts—it is to speaking in **different** tongues.
Again, there is an implication in this text that those
different tongues are actually understood by some
of the listeners, at least, without an interpreter.
Finally, there is no distinction here but, rather, a
close bond between glossolalia and prophecy. The
wonderful works of God, the usual object of prophecy,
are spoken of in different tongues by the apostles.
The word "prophecy" is not actually used by Luke,

but we must bear in mind the fact that, in writing these lines, he was thinking of the long quotation from Joel 3:1-5 with which Peter's discourse opens. It seems certain, in any case, that the events described here constitute in Luke's eyes the fulfillment of the prophet's words: "On those days your sons (and daughters) shall prophesy" (Joel 3:1; Acts 2:17). Moreover, Luke himself states, "This is what was spoken of by the prophet" and not the result of early morning inebriation (2:15-16).

The Old Testament text, added to what Luke knew (and probably failed to appreciate fully) of glossolalia in the churches, gives a fair appreciation of the Pentecost account. Whether by using his freedom as an author, or by conforming more or less closely to the facts with which he was informed, or again, most likely, whether by extrapolating and reinterpreting relatively common occurrences in the early churches, Luke certainly intends to consider as a single charism the double gift of prophecy and glossolalia, reducing the latter to a minimum and granting the former a scope worthy of the event of Pentecost. According to every hypothesis, his aim was to attest concretely to the missionary universalism of the Church. By guaranteeing that from the day of Pentecost onward their word would be addressed to all nations under heaven in their own tongues, Luke makes the apostles messengers of the Good News to the ends of the earth. This presentation symbolizes the dispersion and the effectiveness of their word under the animation of the new Spirit.

Note 7.   The List of Peoples in Acts 2:9-11

Before any consideration of the doctrinal interest of the list of peoples in the Pentecost account, a short word must be said concerning the various technical problems it raises for the exegete. It might also be said that many of these problems remain unsolved.

1. Technical Problems Raised by the List

The first of these problems stems from literary criticism. The list presents all the characteristics of a foreign corpus inserted more or less haphazardly at the place it now occupies. It breaks the rhythm of the account and forces Luke to repeat rather awkwardly in verses 11b-12 what he had expressed in verses 6-7. Is this insertion Luke's own work, or that of a later editor-compiler?

The examination of the manuscript tradition and the philological examination of the context and transitional verses do not allow us to deny the insertion to Luke. Moreover, the doctrinal interest, further commented in a later section, fits so well into the over-all theology of Acts as to favor its authenticity. But to determine whether the list itself is Luke's work or a prefabrication is another question. In its present state it certainly presents some bizarre characteristics. It starts simply enough with four nations (Parthians, Medes, Elamites, inhabitants of Mesopotamia) in an East-West dispersion, but the mention of Judea is absurd. The list then bogs down in a morass of minor provinces in Asia Minor (e.g., Pamphylia) coupled with great land masses (e.g., Asia), but omitting countries of major importance (e.g., Syria). Greece is not mentioned, but the Cyrenian desert in Libya is. The Romans come in after they are no longer expected, followed by a listing based on religion—Jews and proselytes, i.e., pagan-born converts to Judaism who accepted circumcision— which is entirely out of context. The document concludes with Cretans and Arabs, both superfluous. Attribution of this jumbled list to the learned author of the Gospel **ad Theophilum** is unthinkable. A better course would be to make its composition the responsibility of an anonymous author from whom Luke borrowed it. We shall probably never know the original context, nor the original format. Is it not likely, in fact, that it was presented differently to begin with? For reasons stated later, Luke may have diminished it to its present proportions—a list of thirteen nations Parthians to Romans, followed by a religious summary, Jews and proselytes, concluded by a summary pairing, Cretans and Arabs, in which specialists recognize a manner of saying "East and West." Some believe the original document to be Syrian, based on the omission of Syria from the list. On all these points, only unverifiable hypotheses can be made in the present state of our knowledge.

2. Doctrinal Interest of the List

The first and most evident purpose of the list is to attest in its own way to the universality of the mission field committed to the apostles. Paradoxically, the inclusion of minor provinces of the empire concurs in this aim. Even the most out-of-the-way corners of the world do not escape the announcement of the Good News. Would it be exaggerating to go beyond this, seeing as Luke's intention the division of the universal mission among the Twelve he has just constituted as a college? This would agree with usual biblical practice.

Actually, the list includes twelve nations united by a summary notion of geography. The Romans seem mentioned as an afterthought. They are the furthest from Jerusalem, and they represent the last boundaries of Gentiledom, toward which the author of Acts is to bring Paul, a supernumerary apostle, whose election also comes as a sort of afterthought, following the choice of the Eleven and that of Matthias. As theoretical as it may be, such reasoning does not contradict the logic of the book.

Another preoccupation to which this list may correspond is more subtle to demonstrate, if "demonstrate" is the correct word. We have seen that Luke must have been familiar with the rabbinical speculations concerning the Voice of Sinai which separated into seventy dialects corresponding to the seventy nations numbered in Genesis 10:1-31. Moreover—a mere coincidence, perhaps?—the book of Numbers mentions seventy elders with whom Moses, at the Lord's command, surrounded himself (Numbers 11:16). The ensemble of these recollections could have had its role to play in Luke's reflection and so have influenced his decision to include in his account a sort of List of Nations. It was merely a matter of reducing the number in proportion to the number of apostles, twelve plus one. These twelve names would suffice for the purpose, just as twelve peoples were enough to suggest the intent to summarize the total **oikoumene.**

This list of peoples plays the same role with respect to the Christian Pentecost as the list in Genesis did with respect to the promulgation of the law. There is a further possible comparison. The list of peoples in Genesis 10 served as prologue to the pitiable story of the Tower of Babel (Genesis 11:1-11). Before its erection, all nations spoke one language, which became diversified to divide men when their pride erupted. This story is redeemed here. The list of peoples used by Luke introduces the notion of all humanity gathered together in a common tongue understood by all. The language used to express the wonderful works of God, the tongue used to proclaim the Good News of salvation will henceforth be understood by all men. At last the Spirit of Pentecost has re-established the unity of mankind.

CONCLUSION

The development of the teachings contained in these pages of the Acts of the Apostles has been sufficient, I trust, that lengthy conclusions may be dispensed with. At the end of this study, I shall merely attempt to justify the title given to it: "The Gospel of the Childhood of the Church."

The second volume of Luke's work is indeed a Gospel. The word may be taken in two senses. First, it designates a particular literary form. A Gospel, in the current sense of the word, is a short book concerning Jesus Christ, retracing the important works of his life and his teachings. Upon reflection, do we not discover that this is the unique purpose Luke has pursued in writing the third Gospel, a purpose which remains unfulfilled until Paul has been brought to Rome? There is no break in the unity of the two volumes. The latter as well as the former is the story of Christ (cf. Acts 2:41, 47; 4:4; 5:14; 6:1; etc.), of curing the sick, raising the dead, announcing the message, and traveling the pathways of the world designated by the Spirit. It is the continuing story of Christ, crucified anew at each crisis to be met, in the persecuted Church of Jerusalem, in the Church of the dispersion threatened with destruction, in the Church of Gentiledom endangered by the hostility of both Judaism and the empire, allied against Jesus of Nazareth (cf. Acts 4:27).

The word "gospel" has another, more theological significance. It is a kerygma, Good News, the message of the salvation wrought by Jesus Christ. In this aspect, too, Acts deserves the title "Gospel." The book undoubtedly speaks no more of the paschal mystery which is to free the world, but of that same mystery which, having freed the world has by the same act constituted the Church of the saved. Acts is the book of the missionary proclamation of the redemption, of the paschal event lived out in the community of the new Israel which prolongs Christ Risen. Of itself, the Church is Good News, a message of salvation. Its very presence in the world is a sensible sign of redemption wrought by the paschal mystery in which it lives. It would be necessary to give a much more detailed commentary extending far beyond the first thirty-nine verses to justify this theology, but what we have read suggests it adequately.

If Acts is truly a Gospel, in every sense of the word, its first pages are also a childhood Gospel, not only because the subject is the birth of the Church, but, more technically, so to speak, because they use literary devices proper to this form of narrative. They have been studied during the reading, and consist in a scholarly and persistent recourse to Scripture, from which a mass of recollections is drawn, refashioned, and amalgamated. To reduce this literary form to a mere collection of texts is unfair, for it requires a profound christological exegesis of the Old Testament. This recourse to midrash is self-justifying. It is no mere witty game to which one abandons oneself for the pure pleasure of juggling texts with no particular purpose.

Luke used this technique on two occasions and for two reasons. First, the vastness of the mysteries he was dealing with precluded conventional modes of expression, which could not meet the measure of the reality to be expressed. Old Testament symbolism, with its simple imagery, and with the importance the faith of Israel and of the Church granted it, permitted many evocations of a profundity impossible to attain by other means. On the other hand, it is also true, no doubt, that the first days of the Church, like those of Jesus, had not provided Luke a well-furnished documentation, recollections having dimmed after a half-century of existence. To make up for this lack of information, midrash is used to express a theology. The account is midrash for the most part, then, bolstered here and there by artfully reworked historical traditions.

The relationship between Acts 1:1-2:13 and Luke 1-2 goes beyond these general comparisons. The prologues of both volumes are conceived similarly, and their purposes are similar. Earlier reference was made to the first chapters of Luke as a sort of micro-gospel, a miniature in which are sketched, veiled and subtle, as a foretaste, the major themes of the Gospel. These themes of redemption, universality, the reception of the Christian message, Jesus' pilgrimage, and the rest are included as road markers of a sort. The attentive reader will recognize them and, eager to learn more, begin immediately to read the rest of the book with a watchful eye. The childhood accounts are a sort of prophecy of the Lord's public life. We are aware that the same is true of the corresponding section of Acts. Luke has wisely announced in about fifty sentences, in the most diverse forms, the basis of his ecclesiology and the themes of his second work, the restoration of Israel, the truth of the apostolic witness, the role and the field of action of the Twelve and especially, the identity of Christ with his Church.

The very structure of this account bears a relationship to Luke 1-2. The prelude of the Gospel is summarized as a promise (the Annunciation), a sign in guarantee (the birth of John), and the fulfillment of the promise (the birth of Jesus). Then a series of episodes follows to enlighten the significance of this birth and to suggest the vocation of the newborn child. Similarly, the Prologue of Acts opens with a promise (the gift of the Spirit, containing implicitly the foundation of the Church) immediately guaranteed by a sign (the Ascension), and the eventual fulfillment of the promise (Pentecost), followed by prophetic details which foretell the nature and mission of the newborn Church. With his genius, Luke treated these identical themes without monotony and without fastidious repetition of the same literary devices.

Circumstances did not allow Luke to make as complete a break in Acts as he had in the Gospel between the childhood accounts and the outset of the ministry. Peter's discourse, linked with the Pentecost

event, completes it, and at the same time, it inaugurates the public life of the Church. It was difficult
to decide between including this speech-program at
the end of this commentary or at the beginning of
the one which ought to follow. I finally decided upon
the second course, if only because of a certain
parallelism between this preaching and that by which
Jesus began in Nazareth his own missionary life (Luke
4:16ff.). It seemed better to keep this sermon as a
general introduction to the Church at Jerusalem, departure point and eternal model for the entire Church
of Jesus Christ.

TRANSLATOR'S NOTES

1. The translation chosen as a basic text for Acts and as a reference text for the remainder of the New Testament is that of the Confraternity of Christian Doctrine, © 1941, 1953, 1955, 1961 referred to in these notes and in the text as CCD). The Greek text is that of the 21st edition of Nestle's *Novum Testamentum Graecae* as found in *The Interlinear Greek-English New Testament,* (London: Samuel Bagster and Sons Limited, 1967). Both English and Greek reference texts for the Old Testament are those of *The Septuagint Version,* also published by Bagster (referred to in the notes and in the text as LXX). Any exceptions to the foregoing are duly noted.

A word must be said here about proper names and about the nomenclature of the books of the Bible. Generally, I have kept the same system of numbering of books and verses noted by Charlier, who follows the Hebrew numbering. Students will realize that the references from the LXX differ from this system. Proper names are usually the "common English form" (e.g., Elijah and Elisha), except in a quotation which uses another form. Again, exceptions are noted.

2. *began to do and teach* (AV); *commenca de faire et d' enseigner* (Charlier); *did and taught from the beginning* (CCD); $\eta\rho\xi\alpha\tau o \cdots \pi o\iota\epsilon\iota\nu \tau\epsilon \kappa\alpha\iota \delta\iota\delta\alpha\sigma\kappa\epsilon\iota\nu$ (Gk.).

3. *to the Eleven* (CCD); *aux Douze* (Charlier); $\tau o\iota s \delta\omega\delta\epsilon\kappa\alpha$ (Gk.). Despite Judas' defection, the apostles are known officially as the Twelve.

4. Translated by the translator. No reference is given by the author.

5. *white fluffy clouds; blancs et fous, les nuages* (Charlier). The clouds referred to in Psalm 18:12 are variously described as "dark misty rain clouds" (CCD); "dark water in the clouds of the air" (Eng. *LXX*); $\sigma\kappa o\tau\epsilon\iota\nu o\nu \ \upsilon\delta o\rho \ \epsilon\nu \ \nu\epsilon\psi\epsilon\lambda\alpha\iota s \ \alpha\epsilon\rho\omega\nu$ (Gk. LXX).

6. *Jude (son) of James; Jude (fils) de Jacques* (Charlier); *Jude, brother of James* (CCD); ιουδχς ιχκωβου (Gk.).

7. *Having swollen up* (CCD, notes); *s' etant enfle* (Charlier); *being hanged* (CCD); ηρηνης γενομενος (Gk.).

8. *Let his habitation* (Acts 1:20, AV); *Let their habitation* (Acts 1:20, CCD).

9. *Let another take his office* (LXX); *His ministry let another take* (CCD); λαβετω (Acts 1:20); λχβοι (Psalm 108: 8, LXX).

10. *Comings and goings; allées et venues* (Charlier); *went in and out among us* (AV); *moved among us* (CCD); εισηλθεν και εξφλθεν (Gk.).

11. The text is quoted directly from the CCD, except that corrected references to *the Treasury* are brought back to the incorrect *the Potter*.

12. *distributing themselves* (CCD, notes); *en train de se diviser* (Charlier); *parted* (CCD); διχμεριζομεναι (Gk.).

13. *different tongues* (CCD, notes); *D'autres langues* (Charlier); *foreign tongues* (CCD); ετερχις γλωσσαις (Gk.).

14. *when the sickle is first put to the standing grain* (CCD); *au moment ou la faucille aura commence a couper les epis (d'orge)* (harlier); *when thou hast begun to put the sickle to the corn* (LXX).

BIBLIOGRAPHY

As mentioned in the Foreword, this bibliography is far from adequate to give a complete picture of contemporary research on Acts. A more complete view, judiciously commented upon, may be found in the following works.

Dupont, J. *Les problèmes du Livre des Actes d'après les travaux récents (Analecta Lov. Bibl.).* Louvain, 1951.
_____. *Les sources du Livre des Actes. Etat de la question.* Bruges, 1960. (Eng. trans.: *Sources of the Acts* [New York: Herder & Herder].)

Grasser, E. "Die Apostelgeschicte in der Forschung der Gegenwart," *Theol. Rundschau.,* xxvi (1960), pp. 93-167.

Among complete commentaries on Acts, the following must be mentioned.

Boudou, A. *Les Actes des Apôtres (Verbum Salutis).* Paris, 1933. (Already rather obsolete.)

Cerfaux, L. and Dupont, J. *Les Actes des Apôtres (Bible "de Jérusalem").* Paris, 1958. (Excellent starting point.) (Eng. trans.: "Acts of the Apostles," in the Jerusalem Bible [Garden City: Doubleday, 1966].)

Foakes-Jackson, F. J. and Lake, K. *The Beginnings of Christianity,* Part I: *The Acts of the Apostles,* 6 vol. London, 1922-1942. (A "summa" which is still indispensable.)

Gonzelmann, H. *Die Apostelgeschicte (Handb. z. N.T.,* 7). Tübingen, 1963. (The most recent German commentary.)

Haenschen, E. *Die Apostelgeschicte (Meyers Kommentar).* Göttingen, 1959. (The most voluminous German Protestant commentary.)

Jacquier, E. *Les Actes des Apôtres (Etudes Bibliques).* Paris, 1926. (Obsolescent.)

Mofatt, J. *The Acts of the Apostles (Moffatt N.T. Comm.).* London, 1949.

Renie, J. *Les Actes des Apôtres (La Sainte Bible)*. Paris, 1949.

Wikenhauser, A. *Die Apostelgeschicte*. Ratisbon, 1956.

Some more particularized studies might clear up one or another point, but any choice is arbitrary. The following list includes mostly works in French.

Cerfaux, L. *La Communauté Apostolique*. Paris, 1943.

_____. *Témoins du Christ d'après les Actes, Recueil Lucien Cerfaux*, II. Gembloux, 1954, pp. 157-174.

Dibelius, M. *Aufsatze zur Apostelgeschicte*. Göttingen, 1951, 1957.

Dupont, J. "The Use of the Old Testament in the Acts," *Theology Digest*, III (1955), pp. 61-64.

_____. "Le Salut des Gentile et la signification thèologique du Livre des Actes," *New Testament Studies*, VI (1960), pp. 132-155.

_____. "L'interprétation des Psaumes dans les Actes des Apôtres," *Le Psautier (Orientalia et Biblica Lovan., IV)*. Louvain, 1962, pp. 357-388.

Menoud, P. "Le Plan des Actes des Apôtres," *New Testament Studies*, I (1954), pp. 44-51.

_____. "Jésus et ses temoins. Remarques sur l'unité de l'oeuvre de Luc," *Eglise et Théologie*, XXIII (1960), pp. 7-20. Retif, A. "Témoignage et prédication missionaire dans les Actes des Apôtres," *Nouvelle Revue Théologique*, LXXIII (1951), pp. 152-165.

Thieme, K. "Le plan des Actes des Apôtres et la chronologie de son contenu," *Dieu Vivant*, XXVI (1954), pp. 407-506.

Trocme, A. *Le Livre des Actes et l'Histoire*. Paris, 1957.

To these I must add an unpublished commentary of Acts by P. Benoit, O.P., of *l'Ecole Biblique de Jérusalem*.

Finally, a few excellent articles devoted to the various sections of Acts discussed in this short book.

On the Dedication (Acts 1:1-2)

Creed, J.M. "The text and interpretation of Acts 1:1-2," *Journal of Theological Studies*, XXXV (1934), pp. 176-182.

Larranaga, V. "El proemio—Transicion de Act. 1:1-3

en los methodos literarios dela historiografia griega," *Misc. Bibl.*, II (1934), pp. 311-374.

Zahn, T. "DAS 3. Buch des Lukas," *Neue Kirchliche Zeitschrift*, XXVII (1917), pp. 373-395.

On the Prior Apparitions (Acts 1:3-8)

De Donkel, E. "Sale Sumpto," in *Ephem. Liturg.*, VII (1933), pp. 101-112.

Van Stempvoort, P. A. "De beteknis van λεγων τα περι της βασιλειας του θεου in Hand. 1:3," *Nederl. Theol. Tijdschr.*, IX (1954-1955), pp. 57-72.

Wikenhauser, A. "Die Unterweisungen des auferstand-enen Christus," *Revista Biblica*, LXXVIII (1955), pp. 117-122.

On the Ascension (Acts 1:9-12)

Benoit, P. "L'Ascension," *Exégèse et Théologie*, I. Paris, 1961, pp. 363-411.

Kretschmar, G. "Himmelfahrt und Pfingsten," *Zeitschr. für Kirchengesch.*, LVI (1954-1955), pp. 209-253.

Larranaga, V. *L'Ascension de Notre-Seigneur*. Rome, 1938.

33. Menoud, P. "Remarques sur les textes de l'Ascension dans Luc-Actes," *N.T. Studien (Beihefte zur ZNTW)*. Berlin, 1954, pp. 148-156.

Miquel, P. "Le mystère de l'ascension," *Quest. Lit. et Par.*, XL (1959), pp. 105-126.

On the Apostolic College and Its Entourage (Acts 1:13-14)

Lattey, C. "The Apostolic Groups," *Journal of Theological Studies*, X (1909), pp. 107-115.

On the Replacement of Judas (Acts 1:15-26)

Beardslee, W. A. "The casting of Lots at Qumran and in the Book of Acts," *Novum Testamentum*, IV (1960), pp. 245-252.

Benoit, P. "La mort de Judas," *Exégèse et Théologie*, I. Paris, 1961, pp. 340-359.

Dupont, J. "La destinée de Judas prophetisée par David (Act. 1:16-20)," *Catholic Biblical Quarterly*, XXIII (1961), pp. 41-51.

Gaechter, P. "Die wahl des Matthias (Apg. 1:15-26),"

Zeitschr. für Kath. Theol., LXXI (1949), pp. 318-346.

Masson, C. "La reconstitution du Collège des Douze," *Revue de Theologie et de Philosophie,*" V (1955), pp. 193-201.

Menoud, P. "Les additions au groupe des douze apôtres d'après le livre des Actes," *Rev. Hist. Phil. Rel.,* XXXVII (1957), pp. 71-80.

Renie, J. L'élection de Matthias (Act. 1:15-26) Authenticité du recit," *Revue Biblique,* LV (1948), pp. 43-53.

On Pentecost (Acts 2:1-13)

Brinkman, J. A. "The Literary Background of the 'Catalogue of the Nations' (Acts 2:9-11)," *Catholic Biblical Quarterly,* XXV (1963), pp. 418-427.

Cerfaux, L. "Le symbolisme attaché au miracle des langues," *Recueil Lucien Cerfaux,* II. Gembloux, 1954, pp. 183-188.

Delcor, M. "Das Bundesfest in Qumran und das Pfingstfest," *Bibel und Leben,* IV (1963), pp. 188-204.

————. "Pentecôte," *Suppl. Dict. Bibl.,* VII (1964), col. 858-879.

Dupont, J. "La Première Pentecôte Chrétienne," (Actes 2:1-11) (*Assemblées du Seigneur,* LI. Bruges, 1963, pp. 39-62.

Le Deaut, R. "Pentecôte et Tradition Juive," *Asemblées du Seigneur,* LI. Bruges, 1963, pp. 22-38.

Menoud, P. "La Pentecôte lucanienne et l'histoire," *Rev. Hist. Phil. Rel.,* XLII (1962), pp. 141-147.

Vanbergen, P. "L'épitre de la Pentecôte," *Paroisse et Liturgie,* IV (1961), pp. 252-262.

Westerman, J. A. "Het Pinsterfeest naar Hand. 2," *Nederl. Kath. Stemmen,* LII (1956), pp. 97-107.

And, of course, several articles in *Vocabulaire de Theologique Biblique.* Paris, 1964.

NOTE: My only addition to the Bibliography is to recommend to students interested in deepening their acquaintance with Acts and its sources The Septuagint Version of the Bible, published by Samuel Bagster and Sons, London. (J.L.S., translator.)